Literacy Centers

Written by
Irene Allen and Susan Peery

Editor

Alaska Hults

Illustrator

Corbin Hillam

Cover Illustrator

Tim Huhn

Designer

Mary L. Gagné

Cover Designer

Barbara Peterson

Art Director

Tom Cochrane

Project Director

Carolea Williams

Table of Contents

Introduction

Use *Literacy Centers* to make guided reading, literature circles, and small-group and one-on-one instruction manageable in your classroom. Have students complete meaningful independent work and still have time to meet individually with each student. Give students the opportunity to apply and extend their learning through independent and collaborative activities. Literacy centers are time effective and brain compatible. They provide additional opportunities to cover the curriculum while also increasing the probability your students will learn the material.

Literacy centers are a powerful way for students to use their skills collaboratively and independently. Research shows that teaching practices typically thought of as appropriate primarily for early-childhood education are proving to be effective teaching practices for any age, including adults. Literacy centers provide students with the opportunity to cover multiple objectives in a single class period that would have taken several class periods to cover separately. Well-constructed literacy centers are also a way of actively involving students in the learning process, thus, increasing their understanding.

Current brain research has revealed many ways in which literacy centers in your classroom support student learning. Consider the following:

The brain searches for meaning.
Literacy centers create an enriched classroom that positively impacts the functioning ability of the brain. They contain a multitude of resources and are a visual reflection of the thinking and learning that is taking place within the walls of that room.

Learning experiences should be relevant and meaningful.
Students apply what they have learned in authentic ways in literacy centers.

The brain does not develop in an isolated way, but rather in an integrated way.
Literacy centers provide integrated learning experiences, which enhance learning.

The brain seeks to make new connections.
Students build on the knowledge revealed in literacy centers. They are one way to create "hooks" on which to "hang" new learning.

The brain is innately social and collaborative.
Students talk, collaborate, and question in literacy centers. Literacy centers enable students to have access to resources and to work with their peers to practice and extend their learning.

Emotion has a strong influence on learning, which in turn impacts attention and memory.
Literacy centers create a risk-free, positive atmosphere for learning. Through them, teachers are able to design instruction and practice in a way that students find enjoyable.

Literacy Centers is a resource of 19 literacy centers (with activity ideas organized by learning modality) designed to assist you in meeting the needs of students in your classroom. Wherever possible, reproducibles have been provided to make center management go smoothly and assist in center setup. *Literacy Centers* offers setup and management tips at the start of each center. Draw from these and your own professional judgment when implementing the centers, and adapt each center to the needs of your students.

Creating the Foundation of Literacy Centers

There are four basic components to remember when implementing literacy centers.

Learning—Students have the right to become proficient readers and writers. Teachers have the responsibility to ensure that they are meeting each student's individual needs.
Use small-group instruction to provide opportunities for students to grow as readers and writers and extend their learning in creative and challenging ways.

Decision making—Students have the right to make choices. Teachers have the responsibility to provide choices and educate students about making appropriate choices.
Provide students with opportunities to practice the life skill of decision making by incorporating choices within the literacy centers. Giving students choices also allows for flexibility, piques varied interests, and increases motivation.

Ownership—Students have the right to share ownership in the classroom. Teachers have the responsibility to help students establish ownership of the classroom.
Have discussions with students about the design, makeup, and tone of each center. Get input from them on the location of the center, the materials needed, the subjects, and options for creating a cozy environment. Sharing ownership of the centers teaches students to share and respect the contributions of others.

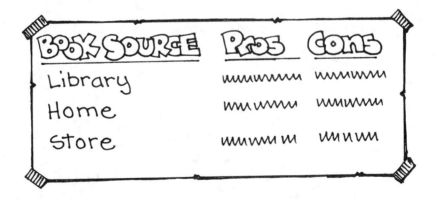

Independence—Students have the right to be independent learners. Teachers have the responsibility to teach independence rather than dependence.
Prepare students for our rapidly changing, technology-based society by teaching them to be active learners who can think for themselves. Present opportunities for students to gain independence in finding resources, solving problems, and determining strategies by creating a classroom environment with established routines and a variety of materials and resources.

Managing Literacy Centers

Determining Center Content

Your first job will be to determine what centers you will create in your classroom. Begin by reviewing the curriculum objectives you want students to master. List all the content you have covered to this point in the school year, and make a note of the information you will address in the near future. Use this list, along with the center descriptions provided in this book, to determine what the literacy centers in your classroom will look like.

Placing Centers in the Classroom

Literacy centers are endlessly adaptable to every variety of space and classroom layout. Create a print-rich environment, and pull from the following suggestions as you design your room:

*   Have students bring center activities to their seats to be completed.
*   Group centers according to noise level—quiet centers in one area and noisy centers in another area.
*   Place the small-group instruction area near quiet centers.
*   Display written directions for each activity.
*   Build centers around already existing areas in your classroom. For example, make the reading center a part of your classroom library, and use magnets to post center menus, directions, and student work on file cabinets.
*   Take advantage of movable furniture. Use bookshelf or cabinet space as a divider, and locate centers on both sides of the divider.
*   Make the most of a small space by using fishing line and/or dowel rods to hang shower curtains or wooden lattice to form a room divider.
*   Post center menus (see page 7) on walls above shelves with center materials.

Establishing Rules and Procedures for Centers

Clearly establish the organization and management of your centers. Preteach your expectations so your students will be comfortable and successful in the centers. Use these guidelines for every procedure you want your students to follow:

1. Explain and model the procedure.
2. Have a volunteer model as you narrate.
3. Correct any mistakes.
4. Have the class do the procedure under your guidance.
5. Correct mistakes.
6. After the class is successful together, have students do it independently.
7. Encourage frequent self-evaluation.

Tell students that while center time is an active time in the classroom, the purpose is to learn and they are responsible for that learning. When a procedure isn't working, problem-solve together to establish center routines that work for you and your students. Remember, only include activity options that students can successfully complete on their own. Do not put a new activity at a center without first introducing it to the class.

Directing Traffic

The next question is how to direct students through the centers smoothly. The following suggestions show how to present available activity options for each center and direct students through each center in an organized way.

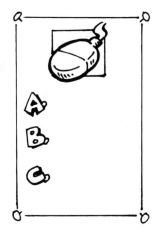

- Photocopy the appropriate icon (see pages 100–104), cut it out, and glue it to the top of a long piece of tagboard. Laminate the tagboard to make a menu board. Use this procedure to create a menu board for each center. Hang the menu board above or next to the center space. Use a washable marker to record on the menu board the activities for that center. Add new activities or wipe away those that are no longer a part of the center.

- Organize students into center groups. A maximum of five students per group is preferable. (You may wish to frequently change the center groupings to allow students to work with a variety of classmates.) Write the names of the students in each group on a piece of card stock. For each group, photocopy on card stock a set of the icon reproducibles (pages 100–104) for each center you will be using. Use the icons to create cards that are the same size as the group name cards.

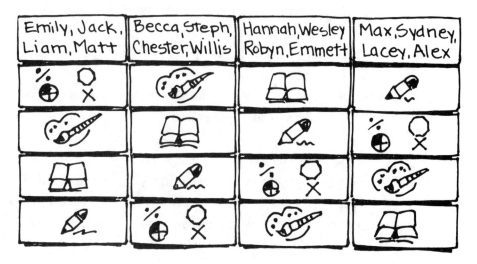

- Next, place the group name cards on a wall or in a pocket chart to create columns. Under each group, arrange the center icons vertically to represent the series of centers, or the path, that students will visit in one day. Each column of the work board tells the order in which an individual group will visit centers that day. Each row of icons indicates where all students will be at any given time. Place centers so students are evenly distributed throughout the room. As you plan the path, consider the time it will take for students to complete activities, and adjust the number of centers accordingly. Each day, move each group's name card one column to the right until all groups have visited each path.

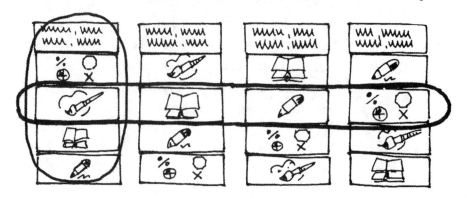

Planning for the First Few Weeks

Introduce students to the idea of centers by starting slowly with just a few center options. Begin with the Writing (pages 26–32), Word Work (pages 41–46), and Independent Reading/Library (pages 61–65) centers.

Introduce one center each day for the first three days by using the following procedure:

- Introduce the center name and icon.
- Explain the purpose of the center.
- Discuss the center rules and the procedures for completing required work.
- Acquaint students with the materials used at the center.
- Tell the number of students who will be working at the center at one time.
- Clarify how the center supplies will be organized.

When all three centers have been introduced, have students practice moving through them. Incorporate a five- to ten-minute share time at the end of the center rotation (see page 10). Ask *What did you learn today?* and *Were there any problems we need to resolve?* At first, much of the learning will be expressed in terms of managing time and behavior.

Use the Skills Checklist (page 105) to monitor the skills you cover in the centers, in whole-class and small-group lessons, and through your other assignments. Check off each skill and date it as the skill is covered through whole-group, small-group, literacy center, or other instruction (e.g., homework, one-on-one instruction). In this way, you can effectively coordinate your content and skills goals.

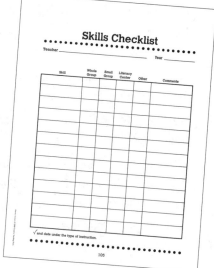

Providing Time to Share

At the end of each day's center time, provide a five- to ten-minute sharing period. Track students who participate in sharing time with the Status of the Class reproducible (page 106). Regularly vary the format for sharing to make the time more interesting. Ask student volunteers to share their work or activities from a particular center, or present students with open-ended questions to answer. Include questions about center content as well as questions about how students evaluate their work habits—both individually and in groups.

You can also use this time to have students give Book Talks, summaries, or reactions to books they have read. Use the Book Talk reproducible (page 107) as a sign-up sheet to plan for student presentations. Give students examples of different ways to talk about books by modeling several Book Talks. Invite them to talk about their favorite part of the book, give a summary, or tell their opinion of the book using supporting details.

Managing Student Work

There are several options for managing work produced in centers. Here are just a few to consider:

- Give each student an inexpensive clipboard to use during center time, or have clipboards available at certain centers.
- Use center folders with one side designated for finished work and the other side for unfinished work. Collect the folders at the end of each center cycle.
- Place a storage crate in a central location. Label a hanging file folder for each student. Place two manila folders in each hanging file folder. Label one manila folder *Work in Progress* and the other folder *Finished Work*. Frequently review the work in each folder for each student.
- Keep two trays at each center—one for finished work and one for unfinished work. Collect the finished work at the end of each day for grading.
- Provide students with a center checklist that they can update each day at the end of center time.
- Use the Checklist (page 108) to implement the crate or trays methods described above. List your students' names down the left-hand column. Then, write across the top the names of the centers for which a product will be due. Collect student work, and check off what has been completed and/or record the grade or rubric number the student earned. Use this checklist to monitor student progress.

Providing for Differences

Clarify your expectations to students, and explain the learning objectives for each center. Make it clear that literacy centers are valued learning experiences and not free time. Provide optional activities, encourage cooperative learning, or support independent reading at each center. If all students in a group complete their work early, invite them to move to the next center early.

Use the following suggestions for students who are having difficulty completing center work independently. These suggestions can also be modified to extend center activities for students who need a greater challenge.

- Use the Status of the Class reproducible (page 106) to manage a student's independent work time. Conference with a student, and have him or her record one or more reading and writing goals on the chart for the day. Review the student's goals and his or her progress at the end of the center time.

- Have students record reading and writing goals for each day on the Setting Goals reproducible (page 109). At the end of center time, have students who are using the form check off any goals they have completed.

- Give students the opportunity to catch up or extend their center activities by designating the last day of the center cycle as a "free day." Do not pull groups for individual instruction.

Monitoring Centers

For the first two or three weeks, monitor students as they first practice and then learn the center routines. Begin pulling groups for individualized instruction when you are able to move around the room for 20 minutes without being approached by a student. Gradually extend the time students spend in centers as they become more self-sufficient. Resist getting involved in the centers. If you find that students seem to need a great deal of assistance or support, ask yourself these questions:

- Did I teach the skill more than once before I asked students to work independently?
- Did I sufficiently model the activity?
- Did I give students a chance to try the activity before I expected them to do it independently? Have students successfully completed the activity or one similar to it?
- Did I clearly state my expectations?
- Did I clearly post the expectations for the center?

Assessment and Accountability

Hold students accountable for their learning and their time on task during centers. Build accountability into literacy centers in a variety of ways to ensure student progress. Monitor this progress and facilitate academic growth by using various forms of assessment. Gear the assessments to complement your school or district grading requirements. Select from the following suggested ways to hold students accountable.

Anecdotal Records

When you are not working with small groups, walk around and make notes about what students are doing. Make notes about work habits, social behaviors, and academic skills. Date the notes as part of a profile for each student. Share your observations with parents at conference time. Here are some ways to manage anecdotal records:

Sticky Notes—Photocopy the Anecdotal Records reproducible (page 110), and glue it to a file folder. Glue a second copy on the facing side of the folder if you have a larger class. Write a student's name at the top of each square, and laminate the folder. Place a small sticky note in each square. Record your observations on the notes, and at the end of the day, transfer them to the appropriate individual file folder.

Computer Labels—Print out a sheet of labels with each student's name on a label. Put the sheet on a clipboard. Record notes for students on their label, and then peel it off, and place it on the appropriate notebook divider, grade-book page, or the inside of that student's file folder. This method allows you to keep notes in chronological order.

Index Card Ring—Make a card for each student, punch a hole in one corner of each card, and put the cards on a large book ring. Hang the ring from a hook by your desk. Periodically jot down observations you make as students are working at centers.

Index Card Folders—Tape index cards in a file folder. (Stagger them vertically so you can see the bottom of each card.) Write a student name on the visible portion of each card (on each side). Flip up the cards, and record the date and your observations.

Rubrics

Rubrics are a useful evaluation tool. It is vital to communicate your criteria to students before they begin any activity. Follow these steps to create a rubric with your students:

• Determine the goals and objectives you expect your students to accomplish at a center.
• Decide how many categories are necessary to describe the knowledge and skills assessed.
• Use specific measurable criteria.

A rubric with five categories and four levels (or vice versa) works well. You can then multiply the total points by five to get a grade on a 100% scale. Turn to the next page for examples of rubric types.

Visual Rubric—Develop a generic, visual rubric system that is applicable to many situations. For example, try an ice-cream sundae rubric.

- A "1" rating is like an empty bowl. The student did not give much effort and the product is incomplete.

- A "2" rating has the ice cream in the bowl. The student showed some effort, but the product is either incomplete or leaves a lot to be desired.

- A "3" rating puts a topping on the ice cream. The student gave a very good effort and the product is complete.

- A "4" rating has all the sundae elements plus all the extras. This student put forth his or her very best effort and the result is excellent.

Work Habit Rubric—Let students help develop a rubric to assess work habits. In the example below, the expectations were suggested as the class established the norms for each center. The class agreed that they should be held accountable for the elements listed on the rubric scale.

Work Habits

Expectation	Day1	Day2	Day3	Day4	Day5
Number of activities I completed:					
*I put things away in each center I used.					
* I took care of the materials and supplies.					
* I was cooperative and shared materials.					
* I used my time well and was on task.					
* I completed all required work.					
* Rate your performance.					

Rate your performance as follows:
1—Not much of an effort, little success   3—Very good effort, but not my best
2—An okay effort, I tried   4—My very best effort

Have students fill out the rubric daily during share time. Invite them to assess five specific criteria on a scale of 1 to 4 over a five-day period.

Product Rubric—Use rubrics to assess the products that students create at the centers. Again, include students in the creation of the rubric to make the assessment more meaningful.

Journal or Diary

Journals and diaries provide another way for students to assess their work. These tools enable students to reflect on their learning in a way that is personal and meaningful to them. Have students write on the Centers reproducible (page 111) a brief summary of what they did in each center they attended on a given day. Have students record this information before they leave each center. Ask students to make a circle in the slot of any assigned center they did not attend.

Center Checklist

A checklist is another way to hold students accountable for the work they are expected to do. Photocopy the Center Checklist (page 112) for each student. Have students complete one sheet every week. Have them write the name of each assignment they begin in the first column, the date begun in the second column, and the date they completed the assignment in the third column. Have students write problems or other comments they may have about a given assignment in the fourth column. Tell students this is where they can write questions or concerns they may have about an assignment when a peer is unable to help and you are helping another student. Encourage them to use their notes to remind themselves to see you before you begin working with other students at the beginning of the next center day.

Portfolios

As you design your centers, plan for products that will demonstrate a student's understanding of the concepts being taught. Include products that will be representative of a variety of ability levels. Be clear with students about your expectations regarding how much collaboration is acceptable. Over the course of a grading period, place each student's products in a separate portfolio, and assess the collected work for a formal grade.

Periodically invite students to select pieces of their work to include in their portfolio. At the same time, make your own choices from their work collection. Use the appropriate (i.e., student or teacher) Portfolio Piece reproducible (page 113 or 114) to explain the reasoning for selecting each piece. For example, a piece that was chosen by both you and the student would have one of each reproducible attached to it. Collect several products over the course of a grading period. Meet individually with students to assess the collection of work, and use the portfolios to assist you in determining formal grades for students.

Centers

Literacy Centers begins with centers that focus on writing skills. Next, there are centers that use reading and writing skills together, followed by reading-focused centers. Finally, a variety of content-oriented centers are introduced. Each literacy center is organized using the following information:

Primary Objective

This section defines the overall objective of the center.

Student Icons

This icon ☺ represents the suggested maximum number of students to have at the center at one time. If you have additional resources available in your classroom—such as more than one computer for the computer center—you may be able to exceed the suggested number.

Center Icon

Look for the center icon at the bottom of each page to quickly find a center.

Setup

Here are ways to organize the center, including where to locate the center and how to arrange your materials.

Management

In this section, you will find ways to manage students and materials at the center. These suggestions maximize student performance.

Additional Tips

This section offers tips to integrate additional content into the center, combine centers together, and make the center run more efficiently. Some centers do not require additional tips.

Resources

Some centers have an added section that lists books, teaching resources, software titles, and Internet Web sites to use in planning, building, and running the centers.

Activities

This section provides suggested activities for the center. Choose those that meet your current needs, or adapt activities to better suit your students. Or, use these ideas to think of your own original activities. The activities are organized by the following learning modalities:

Verbal/Linguistic—all forms of working with language, including the ability to read, write, speak, listen to, and understand the words of another person and what they intend to communicate.

Visual/Spatial—everything we see: all shapes, patterns, designs, colors, and textures; both concrete and in our imagination, including our capacities to visualize and dream. This also includes the relationships and placement of objects in the space/time continuum.

Bodily/Kinesthetic—the full range of movement that is possible in and through the body, including that which has been achieved with the body.

Logical/Mathematical—the pattern-seeking intelligence. This initially involves a manipulation of and play with a variety of concrete objects in the world around us. At the Pure Math and Symbolic Logic level, there is a focus on rational patterns, harmonious designs, and logical-analytical processes.

Interpersonal—human relationships, collaboration with others, and learning from and about other people.

Intrapersonal—the ability to reflect on the self and to learn from our reflection.

Musical/Rhythmic—the whole realm of sound and vibration; sounds and vibrations from the natural and/or humanly created environment, from machines, from musical and percussion instruments, as well as those produced by the human vocal chords.

Naturalistic—recognition, appreciation, and understanding of the natural world.

Not all centers have activities for all modalities. Select from the different types of activities to provide students with diverse learning choices.

Write around the Room

Primary Objective

Students will locate and record spelling patterns and develop new vocabulary.

Have students read and record print found in their classroom environment, including available books. Plan tasks based on students' needs and ability levels. Use this center to follow up direct instruction from whole-class lessons.

Setup

- No additional space is required for this center. Have students complete the activities as they move quietly around the room or are seated at their desks.
- Eliminate time lost to searching for materials by using yarn to connect pencils or pens to clipboards.
- Provide students with clipboards on which to write as they move about the classroom. Store the clipboards on hooks or nails or in a basket or a plastic tub.

Management

- Clarify with students whether or not they may work with a partner.
- If you invite students to work in pairs, be clear with them about how much talking is appropriate to complete the activities.

Additional Tips

- Use the lists students develop at this center to prepare word sorts for the Pocket Chart Center (pages 51–54) or the Word Work Center (pages 41–46).
- This center can be incorporated into the Word Work Center.

Activities
Verbal/Linguistic

- Have students locate and record words that
    rhyme
    contain a targeted "chunk" (e.g., *-tion*)
    have the same vowel sound
    have the same vowel pattern
    have a specific number of syllables
    contain prefixes or suffixes
    are synonyms
    have more than one meaning
    are homonyms
    are antonyms
    are different parts of speech

- Give students the Word Families reproducible (page 115), and invite them to discuss how each word in a given word family (e.g., *aud*) is similar to and different than the other words in that family. Challenge them to think of two new words for each family. Then, have them choose a word, define its root word, and generate four more words with the same root word. Invite pairs of students to share the words they generated and tell the meaning of their root word. Have students use a dictionary to check their guesses.

Bodily/Kinesthetic

- Give students a copy of the appropriate Scavenger Hunt reproducible (page 116 or 117). Have students sort words by their function (e.g., writing *sink* under the *Nouns* category) on the Scavenger Hunt for Word Use reproducible (page 116). Fill in the name and category heads of the content area, unit subject, or theme (see illustration) on the Scavenger Hunt by Topic reproducible (page 117) and then make copies

for students. Have students locate words in the classroom that fit each category. For both reproducibles, ask students to list a specific number of words, and then challenge them to find additional words.

- Cut small index cards into five 3" (7.5 cm) long pieces. Have students copy the words from a classroom word list onto the index card pieces. Invite them to sort their words according to your suggested rule or pattern (or to discover their own patterns in the group of words). Have students record their results on the Word Sort reproducible (page 118).

Computer Literacy

Primary Objective

Students will use a variety of strategies to acquire information from electronic resources, with appropriate supervision.

Give students an opportunity to practice computer skills and explore the wide variety of uses for the computer. Enhance learning by giving students the chance to work with different software titles and the Internet.

Setup

- List the options available on each computer on posterboard or chart paper. Add to the menu as new software is introduced.
- Organize all software titles alphabetically, and store them upright in a shoe box. Use index cards labeled at the top with each letter to divide the software. Keep a master list of all the software titles near the box for students to browse.

Management

- Before anything else, check your district's computer-use policies to be sure your plans are in alignment with those policies.
- If parent permission forms are required for Internet access, obtain, distribute, and collect them before providing students with access to the Internet. Even if your district does not require them, you may want to obtain written permission from parents. Send a note to parents describing your policies and intentions, and have parents sign and return it. Be sure to include consequences you set for students who do not follow your policies.

- Use a minute timer to indicate the amount of time a student has on the computer.
- Preview Web sites before inviting students to browse them. Bookmark approved sites on your Internet browser, and invite students to view only the approved sites.

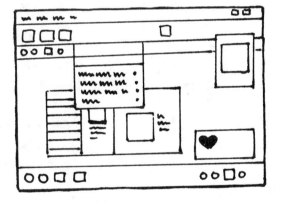

- Introduce software one program at a time to ensure independence in this center. If available at your school, use a projector or large screen TV that connects to the computer and facilitates viewing of the computer screen by the entire class. If this is not available, introduce software in small groups.
- Have students work in pairs. Have one student watch and/or coach while the other works. Have students switch roles at regular intervals.

Additional Tip

- Designate one or two students as "Computer Experts." Teach these students to assist other students when problems arise. Have them be responsible for making sure the computer gets turned on and off correctly, that the printer has paper, and that students move easily between different software titles.

Activities
Verbal/Linguistic

- Have students experiment with various features on a word-processing program to publish a piece of their writing. Encourage students to try different fonts, colors of print, clip art, and margin sizes.

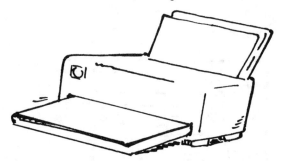

- Have students use books with accompanying CDs, such as the World Book Interface series. Explain to students that they must read the books to be able to play the games.

- Set up a classroom Web site for students to publish their writing. Design the site to function as a class newsletter, and encourage parents to check the site at home with their child. Another option would be to post an interactive "Question-of-the-Week" on the Web site. Work with students to compile the answers and regularly review them. (As with any Internet material, review answers prior to allowing students to view them.)

Visual/Spatial

- Have students use programs such as Hyperstudio to develop multimedia projects.

- Have students choose a game to play from the available software.

- Have students use the on-line or CD encyclopedia or on-line magazine articles to research a topic they are currently studying.

- Invite students to use the Internet to investigate sites that correlate to a theme or novel study. (See Resources on page 23.) Encourage students to gather information from these sites and describe the information in a paragraph.

Interpersonal

- Invite students to e-mail other students within your schoolwide e-mail system. Use the e-mail as the basis for cross-grade-level projects.

- Develop business partnerships in which employees mentor students through e-mail. Closely monitor this activity, and always follow district policy to ensure the safety of all students.

- Have students collaborate to produce an article for the class newsletter on an assigned or self-selected subject. Have groups add their completed, edited article to the master document. Print out the finished newsletter on a Friday, photocopy it, and send it home to parents.

Resources

101 Things to Do on the Internet by Mark Wallace (EDC Publishing)

Online KIDS: A Young Surfer's Guide to Cyberspace, rev. ed., by Preston Gralla (John Wiley & Sons)

Suggested Web Sites

The following sites were found to be functional, child friendly, and child safe at the time of publication, but all sites should be checked by a responsible adult before directing students to them. Going to a site, bookmarking it, and then directing students to the bookmark is the safest way to encourage students to explore these sites. Some of the sites require Shockwave to function properly. This program can be downloaded at the shockwave site at www.Shockwave.com at no cost.

www.pbskids.org/

The games and activities on the PBS Kids site are engaging and age appropriate, but linked to PBS children's programming. The site also contains a fact-based trivia game and links to many other education-related sites.

www.kidscom.com/

The motto of the KidsCom site is "Play Smart, Stay Safe, Have Fun." Students can send C-cards, post messages on current topics, and participate in the "Graffiti Wall Chat"—monitored by KidsCom staffers. Students must register to chat by filling out a hard-copy form that a parent/guardian must sign and then fax or mail to KidsCom.

www.howstuffworks.com/

The How Stuff Works site contains a great deal of information to fascinate an eight- to ten-year old. Students may need some assistance when using the site. The best features of the site are the list of top 10 questions (e.g., How do light sabers work? What causes flatulence? Is flour inflammable?) and the top 10 articles (e.g., How Do Car Engines Work? How Do Telephones Work? How Does Television Work?).

brainquest.com/

The Brain Quest Clubhouse site requires Shockwave in order to function properly. Students can send e-postcards, play games, answer grade-specific questions, and discover delicious recipes such as the "Brain Shake"—a yogurt/fresh fruit smoothie.

www.kids-space.org

Some of the elements of the Kids' Space site require Shockwave. This Web site's motto is "Of Kids, By Kids, For Kids," and it really seems to live up to its promise! This site includes delightful activities that invite students to be creative in a supportive peer community. The first sentence of their mission statement is "Kids' Space was created to foster literacy, artistic expression, and cross-cultural understanding among the world's children."

artsafari.moma.org

At the Art Safari site students can click on a picture of a great work of art and follow the prompts to create their own story about the picture. Then they can title their story and post it to the site's story gallery. They can also create "fantastic animals" in a nifty draw/paint program that allows users to choose from a variety of imaginative shapes, fill them with various colors/patterns, and then rotate, move, and enlarge the shapes. Students can also view art and sculpture.

www.brainbinders.com/

The Brain Binders site contains tons of print-and-fold brain teaser puzzles. Choose your preferred level of difficulty (e.g., two fold, three fold), print out the puzzle, and have students test their problem-solving skills.

www.trustkids.org/

Trusty's Kids Corner is sponsored by the National Trust for Historic Preservation. Students can view photos of an old building and submit paragraphs or sketches of how they would save it. There are other opportunities for students to identify and write about old buildings in their own towns. The site offers monthly T-shirt prizes and the winners are featured in a showcase on the site. The puzzles and games require Shockwave.

www.geocities.com/EnchantedForest/5165

The K–12 Integrated Internet Projects site features "Poetry Pals—the K–12 Student Poetry Publishing Project." It is targeted at students internationally, so students can read poetry written by children in other languages (but always translated into English). In order to participate, students must read and agree to the site rules. Site editors review all material and remove any deemed inappropriate.

www.supersurf.com/

This is the World Surfari site. It features in-depth explorations of 19 countries around the world (e.g., Gibraltar, Sweden, Qatar, Greece). Information is included for each country under the following categories: People, History, Culture, and What's New?

www.playmusic.org

This is the American Symphony Orchestra League's extremely kid-friendly "get acquainted with the orchestra" site. This site requires Shockwave to function properly. A student conductor welcomes students and takes them to a stage, where they can click on any "family" of orchestra instruments. Games include connecting a sound with its instrument, putting a broken instrument back together, and matching/repeating rhythms. The site also contains lots of great classical music sound bytes.

 # Writing

Primary Objective

Students will write for a variety of audiences and purposes and in various forms, applying their knowledge of grammar and usage.

Provide students with an opportunity to explore and practice their own creative writing abilities and to independently apply writing skills taught in formal writing instruction such as guided writing or writing workshop mini-lessons.

Setup

- Design the Writing Center to be a clearly defined, attractive, well-organized area of the room.
- Any arrangement of furniture that provides students with a comfortable writing space, free of distractions, will work. Stock shelves or portable plastic tubs with paper of various sizes, shapes, and colors; patterns for shape books; colored pens and markers; standard and decorative scissors; and other materials for publishing student writing.

- Organize and clearly label materials. Students will be able to independently access the materials and will be more likely to clean up after they finish working.
- Frequently model handling and storing all materials, especially tools.

Management

- Create student portfolios to store work samples throughout the year. Train students to select and evaluate their own writing. (For more information, see the section on Portfolios on page 16.) Use the portfolios to determine a student's writing grade and as a way to share student growth during parent/teacher conferences
- Provide a system for storing works in progress, such as hanging folders in a crate or easily accessible pocket folders. Also create a clearly defined place for students to turn in published pieces.

Additional Tips

- Most products from this center are of first-draft quality due to the limited time. They will assist students in gaining writing fluency. To have students further develop the topics, encourage them to build on these first drafts in future writing workshops.
- Include student drafts in writing workshop as a revision lesson (but do not share author names without permission). Ask students to revise these drafts at the center.
- Provide time for students to share their completed work with others. Encourage students to go to their peers for feedback as they work.
- Provide a "fizzle box" or a storage place for discontinued pieces. Encourage students to periodically check their folder in the fizzle box to see if new interest is sparked in the abandoned piece.
- Keep a basket of laminated pictures available in the center. Old calendars are an excellent source of interesting ones. Invite students to use the pictures as a resource when looking for a new writing topic.

Activities
Verbal/Linguistic

- Write simple noun-verb sentences on sentence strips, and laminate them. Display the simple sentences on a bulletin board titled *Vivid Writing*. Have students elaborate on each sentence, adding descriptive vocabulary and replacing overused words such as *liked* with more specific verbs such as *adored*. Have them write their finished sentences on colored sentence strips, and post each new sentence near the original sentence on the bulletin board. Encourage students to read their own writing pieces to find bland writing to revise at the center.

- Label sheets of chart paper with headings for each of the senses. Have students brainstorm descriptive words for each sense (e.g., *cold, clammy* for touch), and have each student write his or her contributions on the appropriate charts. Invite students to look for ideas in library books, thesauruses, and textbooks. Edit the lists as a class at a later time, and ask volunteers to compile the completed lists in a class thesaurus. Keep it in the Writing Center for student reference and additions.

- Make "sentence stubs" by writing story starters on small strips of colored paper. Keep the stubs in a coffee can at the center. Invite students to select a stub and write for 15 to 20 minutes without stopping. The resulting paragraph or story is their finished product.

- Invite students to use center time to follow up on projects they started during the writing period.

- Assign each student a letter of the alphabet and a corresponding word to fit a theme. Have students write a paragraph summarizing the information they found about that word and illustrate their page for a class ABC book. Jerry Pallotta's alphabet books are an excellent example of these "big kid" ABC books. (See Resources, page 31.)

- Have each individual in a center group start a story. At the end of the center time, invite the group members to place their unfinished story in a folder labeled for their group. The next day, have each member of the group pull another student's writing from the folder and continue the story. Have students continue this practice until all students have written part of each story in the group folder. Share the finished stories with the class.

Visual/Spatial

- Photocopy the Brainstorming reproducibles (pages 119–123) on colored paper, and invite students to choose one for that day. Encourage students to try a different brainstorming reproducible for each day they are at the center in that cycle. Invite them to use one of the completed brainstorming reproducibles to help them write their next first draft during their writing period.

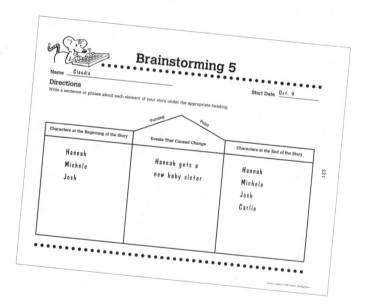

- Provide students with small or medium sticky notes. Have them write each detail for their topic on a separate sticky note and then arrange the sticky notes in outline order on a piece of construction paper. Invite them to use the finished prewrite to help them write their next first draft during their writing period.

- Have students create a story from a picture prompt. Display the finished pieces with the original picture.

- Have students begin by creating a great antagonist or a villainous character. Have them use the Most Wanted reproducible (page 124) to fully develop their character. Then, invite students to write a story about this character.

Bodily/Kinesthetic

- Feature a specific type of book (e.g., pop-up book, flip book) in the center. Have each student choose a topic and create that type of book. After you introduce several types, invite students to choose what type of book to publish.

Interpersonal

- Have students write a letter to a celebrity. Get addresses from *The Kid's Address Book* by Michael Levine, and write them on a chart. Provide envelopes and lined paper. Send the completed letters and wait for the responses!

- Have students develop secret codes and use them to write messages to you or their classmates.

- Write an open-ended question to which students respond. Tell students how long you expect their answer to be.

- Post a message board in the classroom. Have students write messages on sticky notes or on small scraps of regular paper and post them for classmates to read. Try displaying the message board in a location accessible to parents, and invite them to read and post their own messages to the class.

- Have each center group write an article about classroom activities. Have volunteers assemble the articles into one document on the free day of the cycle. Photocopy the articles, and send them home for parents to enjoy.

- Have students use the Writing Center to make invitations to Open House or special events, thank-you notes to guest speakers and helpers, and birthday or encouragement cards.

Intrapersonal

- Have students create their own text innovations—a new piece of writing based on the pattern of an existing piece—as an ongoing project. For example, to encourage students to list descriptive details of a topic and then identify the most important detail, invite them to write a text innovation of *The Important Book* by Margaret Wise Brown. (See other suggested titles in the Resources section.)

- Make a "think box" out of a decorated plastic container. Fill the container with open-ended questions on index card halves. Have students respond to the questions in their writing journals. Consider using a published book of writing prompts such as *Developing Writing Fluency* by June Hetzel for ideas.

Resources

Pattern Books for Text Innovations
Fortunately by Remy Charlip (Aladdin)

A Hole Is To Dig by Ruth Krauss (HarperCollins)

The Important Book by Margaret Wise Brown (Harper Trophy)

It Looked Like Spilt Milk by Charles Shaw (HarperCollins)

Alphabet Books
The Accidental Zucchini: An Unexpected Alphabet by Max Grover (Harcourt Brace)

The Airplane Alphabet Book by Jerry Pallotta (Charlesbridge Publishing)
Also:
> *The Bird Alphabet Book*
> *The Desert Alphabet Book*
> *The Dinosaur Alphabet Book*
> *The Extinct Alphabet Book*
> *The Flower Alphabet Book*
> *The Frog Alphabet Book*
> *The Furry Animal Alphabet Book*
> *The Icky Bug Alphabet Book*
> *The Jet Alphabet Book*
> *The Ocean Alphabet Book*
> *The Underwater Alphabet Book*
> *The Yucky Reptile Alphabet Book*

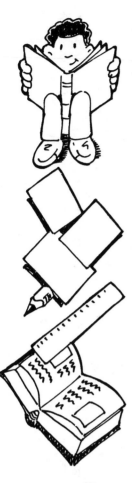

Alphabet City by Stephen T. Johnson (Puffin)

Basketball ABC by Florence Cassen Mayers (H. N. Abrams)

City Seen from A to Z by Rachel Isador (Greenwillow Books)

Cowboy Alphabet by James Rice (Pelican)

From Acorn to Zoo and Everything in Between in Alphabetical Order
by Satoshi Kitamura (Farrar Strauss & Giroux)

Halloween ABC by Eve Merriam (Aladdin)

Prairie Primer A to Z by Caroline Stutson (Dutton Children's Books)

Q Is for Duck: An Alphabet Guessing Game by Mary Elting and Michael Folsom
(Houghton Mifflin/Clarion Books)

Tomorrow's Alphabet by George Shannon (Greenwillow Books)

V for Vanishing: An Alphabet of Endangered Animals by Patricia Mullins
(HarperCollins)

Letter Writing

Dear Rebecca, Winter is Here by Jean Craighead George (HarperCollins)

The Jolly Postman or Other People's Letters by Janet and Allan Ahlberg
(Little, Brown & Co.)

The Kid's Address Book by Michael Levine (Berkeley Publishing Group)

Pooh's Letters from the Hundred Acre Wood by A. A. Milne (Penguin)

Stringbean's Trip to the Shining Sea by Vera B. and Jennifer Williams
(William Morrow & Co.)

Yours Truly, Goldilocks by Alma Flor Ada (Atheneum)

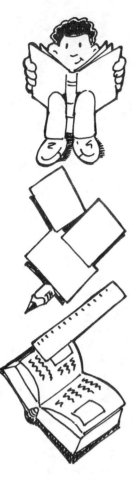

Writing Stories

Arthur Writes a Story by Marc Brown (Little, Brown & Co.)

Aunt Isabel Tells a Good One by Kate Duke (Penguin)

Author: A True Story by Helen Lester (Houghton Mifflin)

If You Were a Writer by Joan Lowery Nixon (Aladdin)

The Moon and I by Betsy Byars (J. Messner)

Writing

Checking Your Grammar by Marvin Terban (Scholastic)

Developing Writing Fluency by June Hetzel (Creative Teaching Press)

Lettering: Make Your Own Cards, Signs, Gifts and More by Amanda Lewis (Kids Can Press)

Putting It in Writing by Steve Otfinoski (Scholastic)

Writing With Style by Sue Young (Scholastic Reference)

Listening/Recording

Primary Objective

Students will listen attentively and engage actively in a variety of oral language experiences. They will build reading fluency and listen critically to analyze and evaluate a piece of literature or a speaker's message.

Stock this center with books and tapes that have previously been read in a shared reading or read-aloud session, or introduce new books and authors through the center. Use books and tapes that reflect a particular theme or genre. Use the center as a recording center where students record either a passage they have practiced reading or an original piece of writing.

Setup

- Provide individual recorders and headsets, which give students more individual choice because they do not have to listen to the same selection.
- Clearly label tapes with the title of the corresponding books. Add a sticker to indicate which side to play.
- Model the correct way to use the equipment and how to store the materials.
- Organize tapes and books in clearly labeled boxes or large resealable plastic bags. If you have closet space, hang the self-sealed bags from clips on clothing hangers.

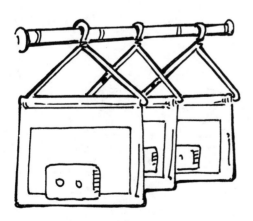

Management

- Model troubleshooting strategies. Teach students to look for reasons why the headphones may not be working, why the sound is too loud, or why the tape is not playing. Teaching students to be troubleshooters will allow you to continue guided reading groups with no interruptions.

Additional Tips

- If a written response is desired, have the Reading Response icon follow the Listening Center icon on the work board. (See page 8 for more about arranging center icons on a work board.)
- If an art response (e.g., a puppet or a picture) is requested, have the Art Literacy icon follow the Listening Center icon on the work board.

Activities
Verbal/Linguistic

- Invite students to choose a book and a tape from the center collection, or have specific books and tapes available for each student to use. Distribute individual tape players and headsets. Invite students to listen and/or read at their own pace.

- Have the group of students listen to a novel on tape. Teach students to be sure the counter on the cassette player is set at 0000 when they begin the book. Have groups record in a log at the center their name, the book title, the page started/finished, and the counter number they ended on. In this way, students will be able to pick up where they left off when they revisit the center.

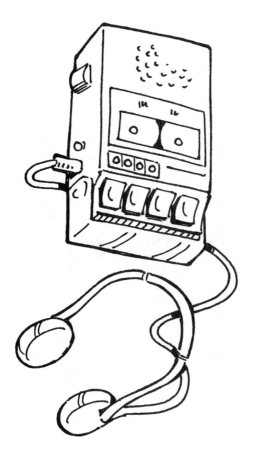

- Have students practice reading aloud a story or passage. Invite each student to record a reading of the practiced piece. Have students begin the tape with the date and title of the selection. Tell each student to record the date, the selection recorded, and the starting and ending counter numbers on a copy of the Listening Center Log (page 125) so that he or she knows where to set the tape for the next recording. Have students avoid unnecessary interruptions by noting problems (e.g., a warble in the tape) in the *Comments* section of the log.

- Have students record readings of their completed writing projects. Provide them with clear plastic bags to hold their tape and a copy of their writing. Place the bags at the center for all students to use.

- Record readings of articles from children's periodicals, such as *TIME for Kids*, *Scholastic News*, or *Weekly Reader*, for students who need extra support. Have students listen to the tapes and complete accompanying activities.

- Have students listen to and follow a taped set of oral directions.

Visual/Spatial

- Have students complete a timeline or sequence of events after they listen to a biography or personal narrative. Have them sequence events on a timeline or create one, depending on their prior knowledge and the level of support they need.

Stellaluna flies with her mother and they are attacked by an owl.

Stellaluna falls into the bird nest.

She becomes one of the bird family.

She agrees to act like a bird.

Stellaluna and the baby birds learn to fly.

Stellaluna is discovered by the other bats and reunited with her mother.

Bodily/Kinesthetic

- Invite each student to make a simple drawing. Then, have the student record directions for reproducing the drawing. Have another student from the group listen to the directions and try to draw the picture. Have the pair compare the results and discuss what parts of the directions were most helpful and what parts were unclear.

Interpersonal

- Have groups collaborate to produce radio plays with sound effects or Reader's Theatre scripts on tape. Have them practice in the Drama/Retelling Center (pages 55–58) until they are ready to record on tape.

Musical/Rhythmic

- When students are preparing to be in a musical program, have them listen to tapes of the songs they are singing and follow along with printed copies of the songs.

- Place tapes of classical or other instrumental music at the center. Have students select a piece and listen to it. Then, have them write a descriptive paragraph that explains how the music made them feel.

- Have students listen to a favorite song and transcribe the words on paper to put in book form. This takes quite a bit of rewinding and repeated listening, but is good for developing listening and note-taking skills. Have students compare their transcription with a printed copy of the song to see if their version matches. (Hard-to-locate song lyrics can often be found on-line. Have an adult volunteer locate the song and print it out for the student.)

Poetry

Primary Objective

Students will explore the genre of poetry by reading, responding to, and writing poetry in varying formats.

Have students explore poetry in a variety of ways. Give them opportunities to read poetry for enjoyment, find poems to use in shared reading, as well as revisit poetry already read in class. Invite students to extend the poetry, look for patterns in words, and learn new vocabulary. As the class is introduced to various forms of poetry and as they become comfortable with writing them, have individuals create their own poetry pieces.

Setup

- Locate this center in a corner of the room. Store poetry books and writing materials inside desks, or keep the books in a container that students can carry to their seats.

- Store poems and books in labeled boxes, crates, resealable plastic bags, or file folders.

- Display or make available in the center directions for writing specific forms of poetry.

- Select many examples of different kinds of poetry. Copy the poems onto chart paper, and display the charts around the room.

- Regularly add new books and poetry to the center.

- Offer baskets of poetry anthologies as well as a basket of books that contain a single poem. (See Resources on page 39.)

Management

- Create a checkout system for students to take poetry books home. Encourage students to share the poetry with their families.

- If you use anthology books at the center, be sure to have at least one book for each student. Encourage students to agree on a method of rotating the anthologies during center time.

Activities
Verbal/Linguistic

- Have each student read targeted poems or poems of his or her own choice. Encourage students to enjoy the act of reading poetry for pleasure.

- As a culminating activity for a content area unit, have students write a how-to poem. Invite students to think about the subject and its distinguishing characteristics and then make a list of actions that personify the subject. Have them begin each line of their poem with a verb.

> Rain Forests
> Grow four layers
> Let sloths swing
>   slowly from branch
>   to branch
> Hold secrets of
>   undiscovered
>   plant and animal life

- Have students choose a poem and think about its main idea. Next, have them brainstorm how this idea could be continued. Invite students to use their ideas and the poem's rhyming pattern to add a new verse. Have students use a rhyming dictionary as a resource.

- Have students interpret the meaning of a targeted poem and discuss their interpretation with the group at an assigned time.

- Have students find examples of similes and metaphors in poetry. Ask them to record their examples either individually or on a class chart.

- Have students take a familiar nursery rhyme and elaborate on it. For example, *The Roly Poly Spider* by Jill Sardegna (Scholastic) is a text innovation—it is a new story that builds on the pattern of an existing story—of "The Eensy Weensy Spider."

- Have students write poems such as cinquains, haiku, acrostics, and concrete poems after they have analyzed and practiced them in a whole- or small-group setting.

> See me with a seed,
> With weeds all around.
> We feed the seed with sun and dirt,
> It turns into a tree.
>   ~Maurice

Visual/Spatial

- Invite students to select a poem and create illustrations to go with it.

- Have students choose a poem, put it in a clear plastic page protector, and label the rhyming pattern with a transparency pen.

- Have students rewrite a poem by arranging the words to create a related picture or shape.

Bodily/Kinesthetic

- Have students choose a poem and build its rhyming pattern with snap cubes. Lines that rhyme get the same color cube. Tell them to use a new color each time a line does not rhyme with any of the lines above it. Then, have students try to find other poems with the same pattern.

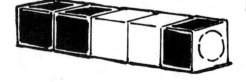

- Have students use commercially produced magnetic poetry kits to explore poetry. For example, they could use premade word tiles to create figurative phrases.

Interpersonal

- Have students browse through poetry books and select a poem they would like to share with the class. Next, have them copy the poem, making sure to copy both the format and the words correctly. Schedule a time for each student to share the poem with the class. Make overhead transparencies of students' copied poems to use for shared reading.

- As a class, have students write a text innovation—a new piece of writing based on the pattern of an existing piece—to correspond with a theme. Have students choose a poem that has a pattern that will work, and then invite each student or pair to write a verse for the class poem.

- Have students select a poem to memorize and then share with the class or a small group when they feel they are ready.

Musical/Rhythmic

- Have students illustrate the lyrics of a song, and then turn their work into a class song book. Either have students pick the song or assign one. Invite students to choose how to illustrate it. Invite students to choose the poem in the Poetry Center and move on to the Art Literacy Center to do the actual illustrating.

- Have students choose a poem and set it to a familiar tune. Invite students to perform their poetic song for the class or record it for the Listening/Recording Center.

Resources

Anthology Books

Angels Ride Bikes/Los Ángeles Andan en Bicicleta by Francisco X. Alarcón (Children's Book Press)

A Bad Case of the Giggles selected by Bruce Lansky (Meadowbrook)

Don't Read This Book, Whatever You Do! by Kalli Dakos (Simon & Schuster)

The Dragons are Singing Tonight by Jack Prelutsky (Mulberry Books)

Favorite Poems of Childhood edited by Phillip Smith (Dover Publishing)

Jaha and Jamil Went Down the Hill: An African Mother Goose by Virginia L. Kroll (Charlesbridge)

Joyful Noises by Paul Fleischman (HarperCollins)

Kids Pick the Funniest Poems by Bruce Lansky (Meadowbrook Press)

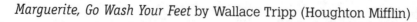

Marguerite, Go Wash Your Feet by Wallace Tripp (Houghton Mifflin)

My Parents Think I'm Sleeping by Jack Prelutsky (Mulberry Books)

A Pizza the Size of the Sun by Jack Prelutsky (Greenwillow)

The Random House Book of Poetry for Students by Jack Prelutsky (Random House)

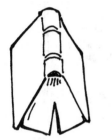

A Swinger of Birches by Robert Frost (Stemmer House Pub.)

Tyrannosaurus Was a Beast by Jack Prelutsky (Greenwillow)

Books That Contain a Single Poem

Birches by Robert Frost (Henry Holt & Co.)

Casey at the Bat by Ernest Lawrence Thayer (Dover)

Cinder-Elly by Frances Minters (Viking)

Hiawatha by Henry Wadsworth Longfellow (Puffin)

Little Robin Redbreast illustrated by Shari Halpern (North-South Books)

Stopping by Woods on a Snowy Evening by Robert Frost (Dutton)

Word Work

Primary Objective

Students will build vocabulary and word-identification strategies through systematic word study as well as increase their proficiency in spelling, grammar, and usage skills.

Include at this center many opportunities for students to work with words, thus reinforcing phonics and spelling skills and strategies. Provide multilevel activity choices to reinforce and extend students' placement in this center. Present mini-lessons on and/or a demonstration of word work concepts before placing related activities at the center. Other activities may be linked to shared reading or writing. Link word work activities to shared reading, writing, thematic units, social studies, and science.

Setup

- Provide a dictionary, a thesaurus, and a book of idioms for students to use at the center.
- Store word work manipulatives in plastic tubs with lids, baskets, or small crates.
- Label containers and shelves so students can put away the materials in an organized way.
- Provide cookie sheets or other magnetic surfaces on which to manipulate magnetic letters, or place the Word Work Center next to a filing cabinet or metal desk.

Management

- Plan and introduce word work activities based upon what has recently been taught and what students need.
- Provide clear direction on how to complete each activity at the center, and describe how and where materials should be stored.

Additional Tip

- For more ideas on vocabulary games, refer to the Write around the Room (pages 19–20), Pocket Chart (pages 51–54), and Puzzles and Games (pages 94–95) centers.

Activities
Verbal/Linguistic

- Have students work on a class thesaurus throughout the year. Put out sheets of paper with various category headings such as feelings. Label one page *Happy*, another *Sad*, another *Scared*, and so on. Invite students to use available resources to find synonyms for the given word. (Other categories might be overused words, size words, sense words, or names of places.) Place the student-created thesaurus in the Writing Center (pages 26–32) where the class can refer to it during writing projects.

- Write questions that require skillful use of the dictionary on 3" x 5" (7.5 cm x 12.5 cm) index cards. Have students choose a "dictionary task card," look up the answer, and write it on lined paper. Provide an answer key in a binder for students to self-check their answers when they have completed all the cards.

- Write a long mystery word on a sentence strip, and cut apart the individual letters. Place all the letters in a "mystery word envelope." Label the envelope with a number or letter, and provide an answer key for students to check later. Challenge students to make words from the letters and also identify the mystery word. Have students record their words on the Mystery Word Challenge reproducible (page 126). Later, invite students to challenge their classmates with their own mystery words.

- Gather books that reveal a specific word work theme, such as homophones, idioms, and word play, and sort them into baskets. Have students read from these books and copy their favorite words or phrases onto a wall mural with an appropriate title (e.g., *Some September Similes*).

- Have students create tongue twisters or alliterative sentences after reading books with examples of these literary devices.

- Make flash cards with vocabulary words from content-area reading. Have students work in pairs. Ask them to write sentences that correctly use their vocabulary words in context.

Visual/Spatial

- Place at the center several large sheets of paper, each with a different affix. Have students brainstorm words that contain those affixes and write them on the papers.

- Have students use a highlighter to identify certain types of words or word parts in a newspaper. They might highlight proper nouns, words with prefixes, or possessive nouns. Have students record each type of word in the appropriate section of the Newspaper Search reproducible (page 127).

- Make a butcher paper chart with a column for each rule you want students to recall. Cut out some examples of each rule from printed materials, and glue them in the appropriate column. Then, have students find examples of the application of those rules in newspapers and magazines. Invite students to cut out the examples and tape them under the appropriate heading. Do not have students glue down their examples until you have checked their work.

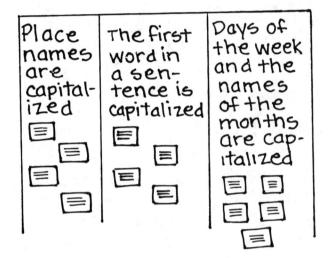

43

- Cut index cards into fourths, and write a spelling or vocabulary word on each card. Cut a roll of magnetic tape into $^3/_4$" (19 mm) pieces, peel off the backing, and stick one piece on the back of each word card. Divide the word cards into sets, and invite students to sort them according to a rule or pattern, or challenge them to find the rule or pattern. (They may find more than one.) Have them copy their responses on the Word Sort reproducible (page 118).

- Following the directions above to make word cards, but write affixes (e.g., *re-, un-, -tion, -ed*) and root words on the cards, and invite students to use them to make words. Then, have students write how the word meanings are related.

Bodily/Kinesthetic

- Write a different statement or question at the top of each of several index cards. At the bottom of each card, write two or three answer choices. Punch a hole in front of each choice. On the back of the card, circle the hole that corresponds with the correct answer. Have students read the question and place a pencil or golf tee through the hole next to their chosen answer. Have students leave the pencil or golf tee in place and check the back of the card. Invite them to make more game cards when they finish the activity, or create cards as part of a whole-class activity.

Use "pick and poke" games to reinforce the following concepts:

when to double the consonant

when to drop the *y* and add *ies* or *ied*

correct end punctuation

correct verb tense

homophones

recognition of correct spelling of commonly misspelled words

fact/opinion

common/proper nouns

types of sentences

- Have students complete sentence-building activities. Label each of five cans with a different part of speech (e.g., nouns, verbs, adjectives, conjunctions). Create color-coded word cards by writing words for each part of speech on a different colored index card (e.g., nouns on red cards, verbs on green cards). Have students use word cards from each can to build sentences.

- Use magnetic letters as a manipulative at this center. Have students

    practice their spelling words

    divide words into syllables

    separate the affixes from the base words

    see how many smaller words they can make from a large word

    build words from a pattern

Logical/Mathematical

- Give students a list of simple, one-syllable words. Have students expand the words without changing the order of the letters. Ask students to add letters to create new words (e.g., begin with a word such as *fat* and create new words, such as *flat*, *flatter*, *flattering*, *fate*, and *fatal*). Have students make a list of all the new words they create.

Interpersonal

- Have students give each other practice spelling tests on individual chalkboards or dry erase boards.

- Have students play Spelling Tic-Tac-Toe where they have to spell a word correctly before they can make a mark on the grid.

- Have students play games patterned after Memory or Concentration where they turn over word cards and keep the ones that match. Concepts like synonyms, antonyms, or vocabulary words and their meaning fit this format well.

Resources

The Dove Dove: Funny Homograph Riddles by Marvin Terban (Clarion)

Eight Ate: A Feast of Homonym Riddles by Marvin Terban (Houghton Mifflin)

Funny You Should Ask: How to Make Up Jokes and Riddles with Wordplay by Marvin Terban (HarperCollins)

Guppies In Tuxedos: Funny Eponyms by Marvin Terban (Houghton Mifflin)

In A Pickle: And Other Funny Idioms by Marvin Terban (Houghton Mifflin)

It Figures! Fun Figures of Speech by Marvin Terban (Houghton Mifflin)

Macho Nacho and Other Rhyming Riddles by Guilio Maestro (E. P. Dutton)

Mad As A Wet Hen: And Other Funny Idioms by Marvin Terban (Houghton Mifflin)

Punching the Clock: Funny Action Idioms by Marvin Terban (Clarion)

Too Hot to Hoot: Funny Palindrome Riddles by Marvin Terban (Houghton Mifflin)

What Do You Hear When Cows Sing? by Marco Maestro (HarperCollins)

Your Foot's On My Feet: And Other Tricky Nouns by Marvin Terban (Houghton Mifflin)

Reading Response

Primary Objective

Students will respond to text to demonstrate understanding and interpretation, support their responses with examples from the text, and connect ideas and themes across texts.

Provide students with an opportunity to respond to what they are reading in the Independent Reading/Library Center (pages 61–65) or from their assigned reading boxes—a box for each student in which you have placed books for him or her to read. The center may be comprised of a reading journal or expanded to include alternative products. Set the criteria for types and number of responses within a specific time frame, but invite students to choose the specifics of how they will respond. Have students choose based on a menu of response ideas.

Setup

- Keep a list of which reading responses you have modeled—written and project based—in your reading and writing direct instruction. To be certain students understand the prompt and project, remember not to add new responses to the center without having students practice them as a group first.

- Invite students to take their journal or project to other locations in the room or back to their seats.

- Use spiral notebooks or composition books for reading journals. Keep the journals together in baskets, tubs, boxes, or inside student desks.

Management

- Have students date each reading journal entry and include the title of the book.

- Do not offer students the option of completing a project as a reading response until they have completed the text. Do invite students to reflect on their reading thus far in their journal, regardless of how far they have read, but keep options limited to a written response.

- Set the criteria for activities to be completed within a grading period or other time frame. For example, within a six-week period, you may require four journal entries and one product. Post this criteria at the center.

Activities
Verbal/Linguistic

- Have students respond to what they read in journals. (This is also a great Visual/Spatial or Intrapersonal activity.) Invite students to write and/or draw their responses. Post some of the following response questions and prompts for students to respond to in their journal:

General Prompts

This book made me realize . . .

This book reminded me of . . .

I would like to ask the author . . .

My opinion of this book is . . .

My favorite part was . . .

This book made me wonder about . . .

Write a letter to your teacher or a classmate about the book you are reading.

List three cause and effect relationships in the book.

Prompts for Fictional Books

Does a character remind you of someone you know? Who? How?

How is the main character alike or different from you?

Why do you think the characters acted the way they did?

Would you want to be the main character's friend? Why or why not?

What was the problem and how was it resolved?

How did the author hold your interest? What writing techniques did he or she use?

Illustrate the setting and use five words to describe it. What clues did the author give to help you visualize the setting?

Chart how the main character changed throughout the book.

How did the character(s) make decisions? Support your ideas with evidence from the book.

I predict . . . will happen next. The reason I think this is . . .

I really liked the way the author . . . because . . .

If I were the author of this story, I would have changed (*aspect of the plot*) because . . .

Create a story map.

Is this story like any other story you have read or watched? Which one? How are the two stories alike?

Does this story remind you of anything in your life? Explain.

Prompts for Nonfiction Books

Some important facts I learned were . . .

I was surprised to learn . . .

I am interested in learning more about . . . because . . .

What information would you like to share with someone else? How would you share this information?

What kind of research do you think the author had to do in order to write this book?

How would this book be different if it had been written ten years ago? Ten years from now?

Create a visual for the information you learned.

Write about the text features (e.g., captions, subheadings, table of contents, index) in or the format of this text and how you used them.

Bodily/Kinesthetic

- Have students use a large sheet of construction paper to create a flip-flop book. Show students how to fold their paper into eighths, open it, and cut to the center fold. Have students illustrate a character on the top of each flap, and then lift up the flap and write about the character underneath.

- Have each student use a 9" (23 cm) construction paper square to create a "triarama" (a 3-D model showing the characters and/or the problem and solution). Show students how to fold the opposite corners to each other to form two perpendicular, corner-to-corner folds. Have students draw a background scene on two adjacent triangles and write about the topic on the back of those two triangles. Have them cut along the fold between the two empty triangles from the corner to the center, overlap the two empty triangles, and glue them together. Ask students to add stand-up illustrations of the topic to complete their triarama. This is also a good Visual/Spatial activity.

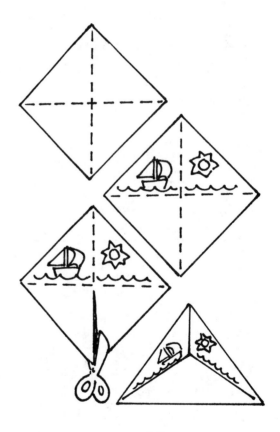

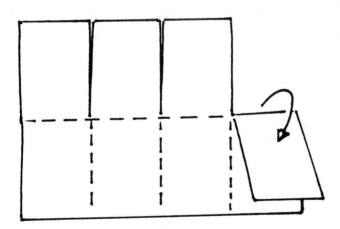

- Have students write a radio advertisement for their book. Invite students to tape-record their finished ads and add them to the Listening/Recording Center (pages 33–35).

- Give each student several strips 1' (30.5 cm) of butcher paper. Have students organize story events on the strips and use them to create a timeline. Invite students to draw illustrations next to each strip.

- Have students use the Venn Diagram reproducible (page 128) to compare two elements of their book.

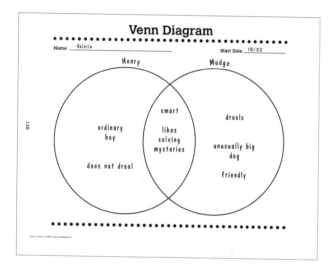

- Have students create a comic strip that summarizes an important scene from their book on the Comic Strip reproducible (page 129). Ask them to write on a separate sheet why they thought that scene was important to the story.

- Have students summarize five key events from the story on the Cube reproducible (page 130) and then use the directions to create a cube.

- Have students draw people or objects that represent a current theme and then write facts on the back of their pictures or on index cards. Use yarn to attach each student's work to a hanger.

- Have students make a new book jacket out of a large rectangle cut from a brown paper bag. Have them fold the rectangle into four unequal parts. The first and last part are the "ends" of the book jacket. Have them tell a little about the author on one end and write a summary of the story on the other. The two large areas in the center are for the front and back covers. Have students illustrate a key scene from their book in the center of the front cover and write the title and author. Have them write a persuasive paragraph to convince others to read the book on the back cover.

- Have students use art materials (e.g., socks, glue, wiggly eyes, yarn, craft sticks, tagboard) to create character puppets for their story. Then, have them write a description of each character's role in the story. Invite students to present a puppet show for the rest of the class.

Pocket Chart

Primary Objective

Students will build their vocabulary and word-identification strategies through systemic word study as well as increase their proficiency in spelling, grammar, and usage skills.

Have students manipulate words and/or sentences in a pocket chart. Use pocket chart activities to provide reinforcement and practice with word patterns, word meanings, sequence, rhyme, syntax, and the mechanics of grammar. Give students the opportunity to manipulate and interact with print in a concrete way by using pocket charts.

Setup

- Attach a Pocket Chart Center to the chalkboard or bulletin board, or move it on a chart rack to different areas of the room. Hang two charts back-to-back to allow more students to work in a smaller space.
- Pocket chart activities come from shared reading, writing mini-lessons, and word work activities. Write text on sentence strips during a whole-group activity, and then place the activity at the center.
- Have students write text on sentence strips and word cards.
- Use a code on the back of each strip so strips can be easily returned to the correct activity.
- Store sentence strips in a large florist's box.
- Make your own storage sleeve for sentence strips by folding a 12" x 18" (30.5 cm x 46 cm) piece of construction paper into thirds the long way. Staple, tape, or glue across the bottom. Label the top, and slip in the sentence strips.

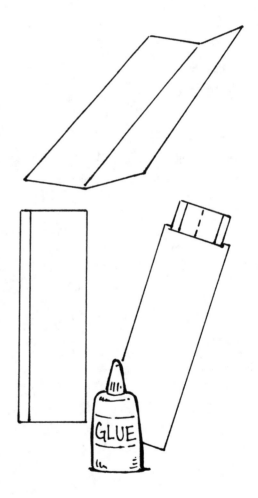

Management

- Have students return all strips to the storage box when they're done with each activity.
- Make activities self-checking wherever possible with this center. Use numbers and colors to code the strips, and write the answers (e.g., *The answer to strip 3blue = He join<u>ed</u> the <u>Minute Men</u>.*) elsewhere, such as on index cards in a file box or in a binder.

Additional Tip

- To reinforce learning across subject areas, integrate the sentence topics in this center with content area studies.

Activities
Verbal/Linguistic

- For timed-test preparation, have students match sample prompts to correct modes of writing (e.g., narrative, how-to, classificatory, persuasive).

- Write sentences that include proper nouns but do not capitalize them. Write capital letters on cut-up sentence strips. To make the activity more challenging, include extra letter cards so that students must think carefully about each word. Have students place the letter cards over the incorrect lowercase letters to correct the sentences.

- Have students practice combining sentences by asking them to choose a correct conjunction to place between two sentences.

- Have students pick the correct case pronoun for cloze sentences.

- Ask students to choose the correct comparative adjective to complete a sentence.

- Have students build words from an assortment of prefixes, base words, and suffixes.

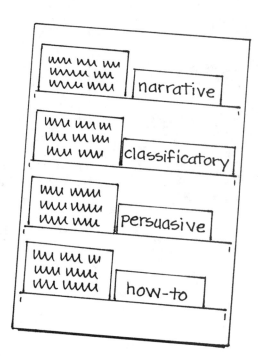

Visual/Spatial

- Have students complete word sorts with predetermined categories. Write the categories and words on individual flash cards or index cards. Have students put the category cards at the top of the pocket chart and sort the word cards by their correct category. Some possibilities for word sorts are

    parts of speech

    synonyms and antonyms

    prefix, suffix, or no affix (e.g., relax, table)

    spelling patterns (e.g., *a, ai, a_e, ay*)

    pronoun case

    complete sentences, fragments, and run-ons

    fact and opinion

    present, past, and future tense verbs

- Have students complete open word sorts in which they categorize a group of words themselves. Add math, thematic, or spelling word cards in resealable plastic bags, and let students determine how to conduct the sort.

- Place in the pocket chart a target picture and a sentence that states the main idea, supporting detail sentences, and unimportant detail sentences. For example, if the picture showed a family having a picnic, one sentence would state that fact, supporting detail strips might include *Mom spread a blanket on the grass for everyone to sit on. Dad drove the family to the park. Dan carried the ice chest from the car. We ate sandwiches and chips.* Unimportant details might include statements such as *The van is brown* or *They live in a city.* Have students identify the main idea

statement and place it in the chart first, followed by the supporting detail sentences. Unimportant detail sentences are left off the chart.

Bodily/Kinesthetic

- Have students use clothespins or pasta to punctuate sentences or direct quotations written on sentence strips.

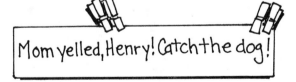

- Have students match cards in a game of Memory or Old Maid with sentence strips. Write a word or a sentence with a blank on each strip. Invite students to find the strip that will match that word or fill in that blank. The following are a few concepts that will work for this activity:

    synonyms

    antonyms

    abbreviations and what they stand for

    content area vocabulary words and their
      meanings

    characters and their traits

    transitional vocabulary (e.g., *first, then, next,
      finally*)

    words that signal cause and effect or if-then relationships, (e.g., *therefore, because*)

    prefixes or suffixes and their meanings

    singular and possessive nouns and their correct
      usage

    similes with the best sentence

- Have students "rebuild" a friendly letter that has been broken down into sentence strips. Challenge them to place each part in the correct position.

- Have students practice spelling words with letter cards.

Logical/Mathematical

- Give students assorted word cards with words representing all parts of speech. Have them use the words to create a short story in the pocket chart. Invite students to copy the results of their "word puzzle" on paper and share the final product with the class.

- Write each step to a recipe or the event from a read-aloud on a separate sentence strip. Have students sequence the sentence strips.

| I will go to the store | because | we have no food. |

| The giant was as tall as ___. | a skyscraper |

Drama/Retelling

Primary Objective

Students will engage in dramatic interpretations that enhance reading comprehension and foster oral language development.

Have students engage in highly productive language activities that may include manipulating puppets, reading and/or writing plays, and dramatizing a story with some suggested costuming (e.g., masks, hats) or simple props (e.g., character figures, doll furniture).

Setup

- Place a chart at the center that outlines the sequence of steps students must follow for each activity.

> Read the script twice.
> Learn your lines.
> Practice saying them with expression.
> Add the movements.

- Have copies of prepared scripts available for student use, and give students the option of creating their own scripts.
- Provide a box filled with everyday objects and clothing items to be used as props and costumes for the student activities.

Management

- Students may need two days or double the time in this center depending on the depth of the activities or their interest level.
- Choose one aspect of the suggested activities, and develop it well with the class before adding another component to this center.
- After sharing stories with the class, add Reader's Theatre scripts and plays to the center over time. Invite students to revisit the center.
- Have students fill out copies of the Show Time reproducible (page 131) to request a time to present. Incorporate presentation times into your lesson plans.

Show Time

Student	Today's Date	Presentation Title	Assigned Date and Time
Nathaniel and Max	Oct. 5	By the Great Horn Spoon	Oct. 5 10:00 a.m.
Gillian and Hannah	Oct. 5	Charlotte and Wilbur	Oct. 5 10:15 a.m.
Marie and Lillie	Oct. 6	Sarah Plain and Tall	Oct. 6 10:30 a.m.
Raul and William	Oct. 8	Praiseworthy and Jack	Oct. 8 10:00 a.m.

Additional Tips

- Have students tape-record their presentations, and then place the tapes at the Listening/Recording Center (pages 33–35).
- To evaluate presentations, consider content as well as timing, expression, gestures, eye contact, voice, and interpretation of character traits. Define and discuss these criteria in a mini-lesson before students begin their work.
- Place the Drama/Retelling icon on the work board following the Writing or Art Literacy icon. This will allow students to write a script or design puppets for use in the Drama/Retelling Center.

Activities
Verbal/Linguistic

- Have students choose a favorite part or episode from a story and turn it into a written script. Have them assign parts and practice their script using a Reader's Theatre format. (Students can then record their performance at the Listening/Recording Center.)

- Have students choose and act out scenes from published play books.

- Have students choose a humorous monologue from a published book and practice it for presentation to a specified audience, based on the opening monologue format of late-night talk shows.

Visual/Spatial

- Have students view a short videotape of a familiar book or story. Then, invite the center group to discuss how the story was brought to life. Invite students to discuss the characters, scenery, props, music, and dialogue.

- Have students create a storyboard for their own play. Remind them to include the scenery and pay attention to the sequence of events.

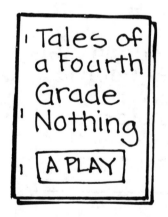

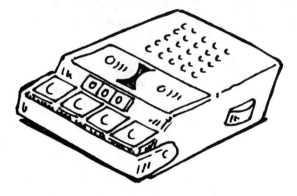

Bodily/Kinesthetic

- Make flash cards of vocabulary words from units of study, and keep them in a canister. Have students draw a card from the can and act out the word for the other group members to play Word Charades. Alternatively, create word cards with character names from read-alouds and other common texts for Character Charades.

- Integrate group charades for science concepts. For example, groups could act out the water cycle, simple machines, food chains, and life cycles.

- After a read-aloud, put a few appropriate props at the center. Have students re-create and retell the story. There can be two types of prop boxes. Have students use one set of life-size props to play the characters. Or, have students use dollhouse-size furniture and props to retell the story with one set of dolls or puppets.

- Ask students to create a talk show with an informal interview-style format. Invite students to take the parts of various book characters and be interviewed by the show's host.

- Find scripts that are related to a social studies theme. For example, during a unit on the Middle Ages, students could act out the story of *St. George and the Dragon*. Place these theme-related scripts at the center for students to explore.

Interpersonal

- Have students plan and perform an original puppet play. Invite them to use one that they created at the Writing Center (pages 26–32).

- Have students act out original versions of traditional folktales. Invite them to use a published script, turn a published story into a script, or write their own version of a folktale from a different perspective.

Resources

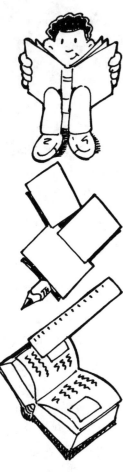

African Americans Who Made a Difference: 15 Plays for the Classroom by Liza Charlesworth (Scholastic)

Favorite Folktales and Fabulous Fables: Multicultural Plays with Extended Activities by Lisa Blau (One from the Heart)

Frantic Frogs and Other Frankly Fractured Folktales for Readers Theatre by Anthony D. Fredericks (Teacher Ideas Press)

On Stage by Lisa Bany-Winters (Chicago Review Press)

Plays, The Drama Magazine for Young People—8 to 10 plays each issue, arranged by grade level, October through May (Plays, Inc.)

Stories on Stage: Scripts for Reader's Theater by Aaron Shepard (H. W. Wilson)

Winter is Wonderful: Reader's Theatre Scripts and Extended Activities by Lisa Blau (One from the Heart)

 # Buddy Reading

Primary Objective

Students will build confidence and fluency and read to engage the listener.

Have pairs of students read a text selection or participate in a reading activity together. Invite pairs to take turns reading or read a selection together. Have two students of similar abilities read together if appropriate, or have two students at different reading fluencies read together. In each case, have students support each other.

Setup

- Designate places for buddy reading throughout the room. Store materials in the classroom library or in a basket or tub elsewhere in the room.
- Store sets of the same book in a resealable plastic bag or in hanging file folders stapled along the sides. Be sure to label each bag or hanging file folder with the title of the book.

Management

- Hold students accountable by having them complete the Buddy Reading Form (page 132). Have students record who they read with, a positive comment about the person's reading, and a suggestion for improvement. Frequently model the use of this form, and offer it for use only after a supportive climate has been established.

Buddy Reading Form

132

Partner Reading ___Zeus___	Partner Reading _____
Partner Evaluating ___Thor___	Partner Evaluating _____
Passage Read ___Jason and the Argonauts___	Passage Read _____
One great thing is ___He reads really loudly. He is easy to understand.___	One great thing is _____
One thing to work on is ___Sometimes he turns the page before I am ready.___	One thing to work on is _____

Literacy Centers © 2000 Creative Teaching Press

Activities
Verbal/Linguistic

- Have students reread an anthology selection with the support of a buddy.

- Include Big Books and chart poems for use in shared reading activities.

- Have students read advertisements, record facts and opinions gleaned from them, and identify the facts and opinions in each ad.

- Ask students to read writing samples and categorize them by genre and/or topic (prompt).

Interpersonal

- Have students read nonfiction books together for the purpose of doing research. Use this activity with a social studies or science theme.

- Have students read a story together and discuss the main idea.

- Have students use echo reading to increase their fluency. Invite students to choose from a collection of one-page passages from familiar stories that contain dialogue and varied punctuation. Have one student read first and the other student repeat or echo what was read. Ask each student to comment on the other's fluency in a positive and informative way. Develop fluency rubrics with the class for use in peer review.

- Have students read passages, newspaper and magazine articles, and brochures and then answer questions. In this way, students can hear others verbalize their thought processes. Also, have students discuss and paraphrase what they have read orally and in written form.

- Give students children's magazine or newspaper articles from which you have cut the headlines. Ask students to read articles together, identify the main idea of the article, and write their own headlines to communicate the main idea.

Independent Reading/ Library

Primary Objective

Students will select and read from a variety of sources for both information and pleasure. Students will read texts at appropriate difficulty levels with fluency and understanding. They will use a variety of strategies to comprehend selections read independently.

The classroom library is a focal point of the classroom, stocked with books and reading materials that meet the students' varied interests and abilities. Keep the center open so that students have access to books for independent reading every day!

Setup

- Staple the My Booklist reproducible (page 133) into file folders or into pocket folders for use as a reading log.

- Display books so that the covers, rather than the spines, are visible.
- Create a quiet and well-lit center. Provide pillows, beanbags, large stuffed animals, inflatable chairs, washtubs with pillows, and carpet mats for comfortable seating.

- Use the following guidelines to evaluate the Independent Reading/Library Center in your intermediate classroom.

Basic
Includes at least one book per student
Is quiet and well lighted
Has carpeting or seating
Has sufficient room for at least three students

Good
Includes at least four books per student
Offers privacy with partitions
Displays some of the books in an open-faced fashion
Has attractive book jackets, posters, or bulletin boards related to reading
Comfortably accommodates at least four students

Excellent
Includes at least eight books per student
Has books organized in some manner
Has a name
Comfortably accommodates at least five students

- Guide students in making appropriate independent reading choices by building in a "choice within a choice." Place books of similar reading levels in a basket. Call the target students together, and briefly introduce the books in the assigned basket.
- Organize the books and materials by author, genre, or theme. Place the books in baskets, and have students label and sort them so they feel a sense of ownership.
- Keep a canister of bookmarks available at the Independent Reading/Library Center to encourage students to read books from start to finish. Books that are not finished can be kept at a student's desk.

- Invite students to use sticky notes and flags to mark pages for specific purposes. These purposes should evolve from direct instruction. For example, ask them to look for examples in the text of characters facing a problem.

Management

- Post rules for the center, and focus on how much discussion is allowed. Clearly outline rules for respectfully using books.
- Give each guided reading group its own box of assigned books. For students who are "learning to read," place at least one copy of a book read during guided reading in the box. Frequently check the boxes, and remove books that have been in the box for a week or two to prevent memorization of a text and to allow other teachers access to these books.
- If you invite students to continue independently reading text that was begun in a guided reading group, keep multiple copies of these texts in the reading boxes so that each group member has access to these books.

Additional Tips

- Assign independent reading books as an extension to content area themes. Have students select a book that relates to what is being taught in other content areas.
- Teach students how to appropriately choose books. Tell them to look for a summary on the back and then preview the chapters or table of contents. Tell them to try reading a page. If they come to a word they don't know, students should stick up a finger. If they have five fingers up before they finish the page, the book may be too hard. If they can read the book in a very short time (within 15 minutes), the book is probably too easy.

Activities
Verbal/Linguistic

- Invite students to browse through the *Barnes & Noble Guide to Children's Books* by Holly Rivlin (Barnes & Noble)—an annotated bibliography—to get a preview of some books they may be interested in. This book includes a section on how to use the Internet to look for children's books. Free alternatives to this inexpensive book are the many catalogs offered by children's book publishing companies. They won't have the information on what's hot now in children's literature, or the extra indexes, but they do offer the color pictures of the covers and descriptions of the stories.

- After introducing a new genre to the class, create a basket of books for that genre. The following are examples of genre baskets:

folktales	fairy tales
poetry	mysteries
biographies	fantasy
science fiction	information books

- Have students use the New Words reproducible (page 134) to record unknown words as they read. Discuss the words during small-group instruction, and have them record the actual meaning.

- Have students read assigned chapters and respond to comprehension questions before the guided reading group meets again.

- If you have introduced a nonfiction text in a guided reading group, have students read additional sections in the same book, or extend their learning in books that pertain to that same subject. For example, if you have brought the group together to teach note-taking skills, have students continue the application at this center.

- Have students create a pamphlet to describe a fiction book they have read. Ask them to list the title and author on the front page. Have students write a summary of each chapter on the following pages. Invite students to summarize the entire book on the final page.

- For nonfiction books, have students produce a pamphlet as they read the text. Have students list the topic, the title of the book, and the author on the cover. Ask them to make a list of what they already know and record some questions on a separate piece of paper. As students read each section, have them record the important information in their own words on the following pages. Have them reflect on what they learned and consider finding more information on the topic on the last page.

Visual/Spatial

- Place books that extend a current unit of study or theme in baskets by level of difficulty or guided reading groups. Label each basket with the names of students who can choose from the books in that basket. Encourage students to write a newly learned fact on a "WOW!" chart—a collection of facts that are new and exciting to the student—posted by the center and initial their offering before they leave the center.

- Have students reread guided reading books from their assigned box. Have them make a timeline for the events in the story thus far.

- Invite students to make a collage to represent a book they have read. Have them cut pictures from newspapers and magazines that symbolize the characters, setting, or other elements of the story. Then, have students glue the images on a piece of construction paper. Encourage students to fill the entire page.

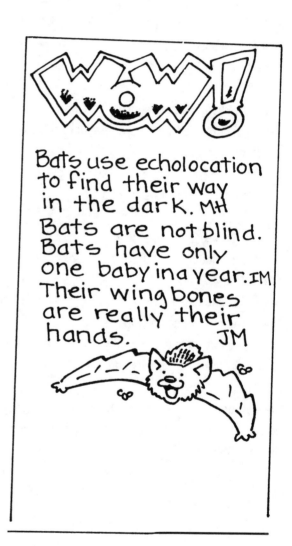

Interpersonal

- Feature an "Author of the Week" in direct instruction during read-aloud time. Label a basket with the author's name, fill it with his or her books, and place it in the center. Read works by the author, and share some biographical information with students. The following is a list of suggested authors:

Chris Van Allsburg
Judy Blume
Jan Brett
Eve Bunting
Betsy Byars
Beverly Cleary
Roald Dahl
Paula Danziger
Tomie dePaola
Jean Fritz
Jean Craighead George
Gail Gibbons

Steven Kellogg
Madeline L'Engle
Mary Pope Osborne
Katherine Paterson
Gary Paulsen
Patricia Pollaco
Cynthia Rylant
Shel Silverstein
Jerry Spinelli
Bernard Waber
E. B. White
Jane Yolen

Intrapersonal

- Have students use the My Booklist reproducible (page 133) to log in before they start reading. Have them record the date, the title of the book they are reading, and the beginning page each day. When students finish reading for the day or time period, have them record the ending page. To foster independence, have students set a goal for the day such as the number of pages they plan to read. When a student finishes a book, have him or her write *end* and use the key at the bottom of the reproducible to rate the book.

- Set goals for the class to reach. Make sure the goals are attainable for each student. You may need to individualize the goals for some students. For example, tell the class to have at least two nonfiction selections on their reading logs.

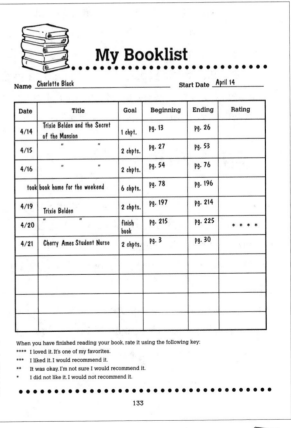

My Booklist

Name: Charlette Black   Start Date: April 14

Date	Title	Goal	Beginning	Ending	Rating
4/14	Trixie Belden and the Secret of the Mansion	1 chpt.	pg. 13	pg. 26	
4/15	" "	2 chpts.	pg. 27	pg. 53	
4/16	" "	2 chpts.	pg. 54	pg. 76	
took	book home for the weekend	6 chpts.	pg. 78	pg. 196	
4/19	Trixie Belden	2 chpts.	pg. 197	pg. 214	
4/20	" "	finish book	pg. 215	pg. 225	* * * *
4/21	Cherry Ames Student Nurse	2 chpts.	pg. 3	pg. 30	

When you have finished reading your book, rate it using the following key:
**** I loved it. It's one of my favorites.
*** I liked it. I would recommend it.
** It was okay. I'm not sure I would recommend it.
* I did not like it. I would not recommend it.

133

Theme

Primary Objective

Students will have opportunities to discover, explore, and construct; use a variety of resources; and engage in predicting, researching, and evaluating as they compare and contrast information related to a theme of study.

Create a Theme Center from any unit of study. Use the center in conjunction with an ongoing unit or after the unit has been completed. Try to use all theme-related materials and activities at the Theme Center, and use generic language arts activities at all other centers. This is especially helpful if you want to incorporate more student choice in your other centers. Create a multidisciplinary Theme Center that employs many components of a balanced reading program, and use it to add interest and motivation for students as they explore a particular topic.

Setup

- Invite students to help decide what materials will be used at the center. Enlist their help in labeling and organizing the materials.
- Place supplies in clear plastic tubs to help students find them quickly and easily. Store small items in clear plastic shoe organizers, and hang them on the wall.

Management

- Store all theme-related materials in large plastic containers, old suitcases, or backpacks when they are not on display in the center.
- Label containers or color-code materials by theme topics.
- List all materials that are stored in a container on the Supply List reproducible (page 135), and keep it in or attach it to the container.

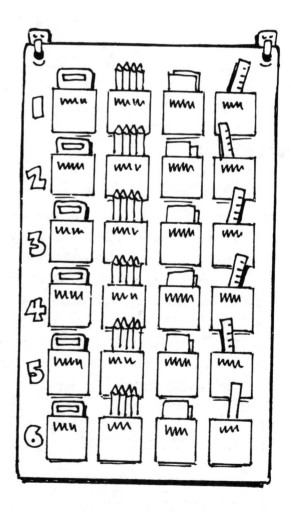

Additional Tip

- Refer to the Writing (pages 26–32), Reading Response (pages 47–50), Independent Reading/Library (pages 61–65), Math Literacy (pages 70–76), Science (pages 77–80), and Geography (pages 81–85) centers for ideas that could be incorporated into this center.

Activities
Verbal/Linguistic

- Have students create a variety of informational books that relate to the theme at the center. Begin a step book as a whole group by giving each student three pieces of plain white paper. Have students stagger the pages 1" (2.5 cm) apart, fold the papers as shown in the illustration, and staple along the fold. At the center, have students label each tab and then add writing and an illustration to accompany each tab title. Suggested tabs include the following: Tab 1—Title and author of step book; Tab 2—*Favorite Word(s)*; Tab 3—*Three Geographical Features*; Tab 4—*If I Went to _____, I Would See . . .*; Tab 5—*If I Went to _____, I Would Do . . .*; and Tab 6—*An Interesting Custom.*

- One way to provide students with a wide range of choices, while still having an opportunity to supervise those choices, is to have students complete a Theme Contract before they begin to work. The contract also has the added advantage of building in accountability and assisting students in planning out their time and resources to meet their work goals. Have students complete the Theme Contract reproducibles (pages 136–137). Give each student one copy of the first reproducible and as many as needed of the second page. Have students number the pages and staple the contract together. Provide a list of four to six activity ideas in each of the learning modalities (e.g., visual/spatial, bodily/kinesthetic). Invite students to choose a total of 10 to 20 activities, and have them copy the activity titles on their contract. Ask them to read the activity directions carefully and list materials needed to complete the activity on the reproducible. This will help students be aware of any special resources they may require in advance. Conference with each student to set realistic goals for completion of each activity, and have students record the dates on the reproducible. Finally, sign and date the contract with the student. Have students check off each activity when they complete it.

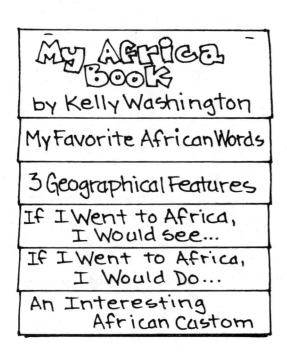

67

Visual/Spatial

- Have students work together to create a class ABC book for a theme. Ask each student to choose a letter of the alphabet, find a related word for that letter, and define and illustrate it for the book. Have the class as a whole group decide on page layout and cover illustration before the book is published.

- Have students create a series of charts and illustrations to show the results of their study. Invite your "experts" to schedule time through you to present their charts and illustrations to another class.

- If a theme lends itself to sequencing, have students show the sequence of events. Have students cut out progressively larger circles, layer them, write each event on the outside edge of a circle (being careful to write the next event on the next largest circle), and then glue them in order. Have students use different colors of construction paper for each circle to make this a colorful and vivid presentation.

- Have students illustrate items related to the theme, label them, and cut them out. Ask students to date each item and write a few sentences about what it is and why it is important to them on the back of the illustration. String a high line of wire or heavy fishing twine from corner to corner of the room. (Space out cup hooks on the ceiling to help the wire or twine stay high when it is weighted down.) Have students put the items in chronological order, punch a hole in the top of each paper, and use a paper clip to hang each item at the appropriate point on the timeline.

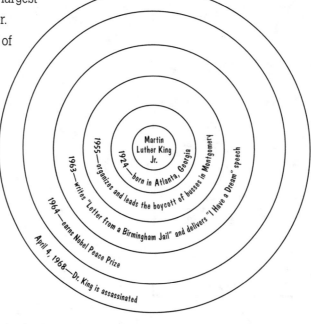

Logical/Mathematical

- Have students generate a brief list of opinion questions related to the theme. Invite them to use their questions to interview 10 to 30 students and then create graphs to show their results. This is also a good interpersonal activity.

Musical/Rhythmic

- Challenge students to poll family members and friends to collect as many songs as they can that are related to the theme. Encourage students to tape-record some of the songs and write the words to any songs they don't know. If the class has access to the Internet, have students research song lyrics under careful adult supervision. Have students schedule a time with you to present their song collection to the class.

Naturalistic

- Have students take a nature walk around the schoolyard under the supervision of a classroom aide or parent volunteer. Invite students to collect artifacts from their walk to use in science-related thematic studies.

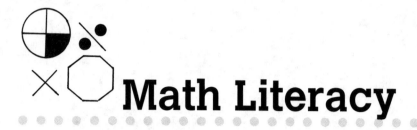 # Math Literacy

Primary Objective

Students will read, interpret, and compute in response to math-related text.

Add this center to your math instruction and hands-on math activities. Engage students in various math activities that involve reading and writing.

Setup

- Include story problems, restaurant or take-out menus, catalogs, cookbooks, and math-related trade books as resources in the Math Literacy Center.
- Use a permanent marker to draw a Venn diagram on a solid-colored vinyl tablecloth or a T-chart on a floor mat.
- Ask parents to donate ingredients for cooking activities.

Management

- Store math journals at this center so students can record their work. Also, have students use these journals during math instruction.
- Develop a recording sheet to document completed activities. For example, if there are six different activities, have students keep a list in their math journal and check off the activities they have completed.

Activities
Verbal/Linguistic

- Place actual objects (e.g., rubber frogs, plastic spiders) at the center. Have students write and publish their own word problems based on the objects. Have students write each problem on the front of an index card and the answer on the back. Tell students to make sure they can solve their own problems to ensure that they have developed sound story problems.

- Have students sort story problems based on key words and operations (i.e., addition, subtraction, multiplication, division) needed to solve the problems. For two-step story problems, invite students to show multiple operations on a Venn Diagram reproducible (page 128).

Visual/Spatial

- Have students construct their own concept books. Give students construction paper, and invite them to cut the pages into a shape that matches the subject. Have students fill each page with word problems or descriptions related to the subject. Topics that work for shape books include

    time—have students use paper-plate pages with a clock on the front

    measurement—have students draw a ruler for the front cover

    place value—invite students to pick one digit, make the pages in the shape of that digit, and then demonstrate the changing value of that digit as it moves from place to place on each page

    multiplication and division—invite students to show their multiple-digit multiplication or long-division skills in books the shape of a multiplication or division sign

    fractions—have students use paper-plate pages to explore equal fractions

- Create a basket of trade books that focus on math concepts. Have students read and record these books on their reading log. Or, place these books in gallon-sized resealable plastic bags with a reading/writing activity designed to accompany the book. For example, after students read *Only One* by Marc Harshman, have them try to think of other options for each page.

- Provide students with picture books that discuss mathematical concepts, such as *The Greedy Triangle* by Marilyn Burns. Have students choose a book, read it, and then use the book to create a lesson for the class. Ask students to write out their lesson and then schedule a time to present it to the class—after you have reviewed the lesson and conferenced with them to ensure their success.

Bodily/Kinesthetic

- Have students follow simple recipes to prepare individual or class snacks.

- Engage students in a "math scavenger hunt" that focuses on one math strand or on integrating math strands. Have students read the clues and then find and record information from around the room. Sample clues include

    1) Find something that is approximately 3" (7.5 cm) long.
    2) Find something that is approximately 10" (35 cm) long.
    3) Find a sphere.
    4) Find the jar of M&M's®. Estimate how many are in the jar.

- Have students measure the circumference of someone's head, the length of someone's smile, the length from their own thumb to elbow, and the length of their arm span. Then, have them organize this information into a bar graph or pictograph.

Logical/Mathematical

- Have students use menus to calculate the total cost of the bill for different orders or choose a meal based on a given amount. Also, have students compute the tip for the meal based on a certain percentage (15–20%).

- Have students use catalogs or book orders to calculate the total cost of sample shopping lists or spend a set amount and compute how much money is left. Try having students compute shipping/handling charges and tax for particular catalog orders based on the corresponding chart on the order form.

- Have students use coupons and grocery mailers to estimate or add up the savings from a set of coupons. Then, have students compute the percentage they saved of the total price.

- Have students construct and/or interpret graphs from newspaper and magazine articles. *Consumer Reports* magazine is an excellent resource for this.

- Use sports cards or the sports statistics page of the newspaper to create questions for students to answer. For example you could ask students to compute averages, percentages, totals, differences, medians, or modes.

- Have students complete logic puzzles or math stories that involve logic. See pages 24–25 for Web sites that contain such puzzles.

- Create a code in which each letter of the alphabet equals a different monetary amount. Write the code on a chart titled *Dollar Words*, and post it at the center. Have students try to come up with words that equal exactly one dollar. A variation is to call the chart *Expensive Words*. In this case, have students try to create words that cost as much as possible. Record student responses on a bulletin board display to show their creativity.

Resources

Cooking

Better Homes and Gardens New Junior Cookbook by Jennifer Dorland Darling (Better Homes and Gardens Books)

Betty Crocker's Baking with Kids (IDG Books Worldwide)

Betty Crocker's Cooking with Kids (IDG Books Worldwide)

Betty Crocker's Kids Cook (IDG Books Worldwide)

The Boxcar Childrens' Cookbook by Diane Blain (Albert Whitman & Co.)

The Kids' Multicultural Cookbook by Deanna F. Cook (Williamson Publishing Co.)

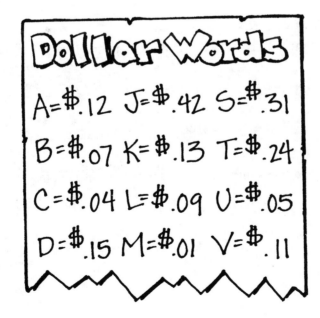

Money

Alexander Who Used to be Rich Last Sunday by Judith Viorst (Scholastic)

Arthur's Funny Money by Lillian Hoban (Harper Trophy)

Bunny Money by Rosemary Wells (Penguin Books)

The Go-Around Dollar by Barbara Johnston Adams (Simon & Schuster)

If You Made a Million by David M. Schwartz (Mulberry Books)

The Lunch Line by Karen Berman Nagel (Cartwheel Books)

Pigs Go to Market by Amy Axelrod (Simon & Schuster)

Pigs Will Be Pigs by Amy Axelrod (Aladdin)

A Quarter from the Tooth Fairy by Caren Holtzman (Scholastic)

The Story of Money by Betsy Maestro (Mulberry Books)

Calculators

Calculator Riddles by David A. Adler (Holiday House)

Measurement

The Dragon's Scales by Sarah Albee (Random House)

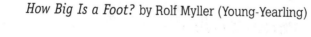

The Fattest, Tallest, Biggest Snowman Ever by Bettina Ling (Cartwheel Books)

How Big Is a Foot? by Rolf Myller (Young-Yearling)

Jim and the Beanstalk by Raymond Briggs (Paper Star)

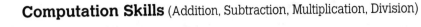

Computation Skills (Addition, Subtraction, Multiplication, Division)

Each Orange Had 8 Slices by Paul Giganti Jr. (Greenwillow)

Mission Addition by Loreen Leedy (Holiday House)

One Hundred Hungry Ants by Elinor Pinczes (Houghton Mifflin)

One Hungry Cat by Joanne Rocklin (Scholastic)

A Remainder of One by Elinor Pinczes (Houghton Mifflin)

Counting Patterns
12 Ways to Get to 11 by Eve Merriam (Aladdin Paperbacks)

From One to One Hundred by Teri Sloat (Puffin)

How Many Feet in the Bed? by Diane J. Hamm (Aladdin)

Only One by Marc Harshman (Cobblehill Books)

Two Ways To Count to Ten by Ruby Dee (Henry Holt & Co.)

What Comes in 2's, 3's, & 4's? by Suzanne Aker (Aladdin)

Time and Timelines
Get Up and Go! by Stuart Murphy (HarperCollins)

Pigs on a Blanket by Amy Axelrod (Aladdin Paperbacks)

Problem Solving
Betcha by Stuart Murphy (HarperCollins)

Herbert Hilligan's Prehistoric Adventure by Paul Epner (Eakin Publishing)

Math Curse by Jon Scieszka (Viking)

Pumpkins: A Story for a Field by Mary Lyn Ray (Harcourt Brace)

Super-Fun Math Problem-Solving Cards by Lynn Beebe
(Scholastic)

Fractions

Eating Fractions by Bruce McMillan (Scholastic)

The Hershey's Milk Chocolate Bar Fractions Book by Jerry Palotta (Cartwheel)

Multiple Concepts

Marvelous Math: A Book of Poems by Lee Bennett Hopkins (Simon & Schuster)

Math in the Bath by Sara Atherlay (Simon & Schuster)

More M&M's Brand Chocolate Candies Math by Barbara Barbieri McGrath (Charlesbridge)

The Usborne Book of Origami by Kate Needham (EDC Publications)

Graphing

The Fly on the Ceiling by Dr. Julie Glass (Random House)

Geometric Concepts

Grandfather Tang's Story by Ann Tompert (Crown Publishers)

The Greedy Triangle by Marilyn Burns (Scholastic)

Shape Up! by David A. Adler (Holiday House)

Science

Primary Objective

Students will observe, discover, read, and formulate conclusions based on experiments and research.

Make hands-on activities that spark curiosity and scientific observation, discovery, and research the focal points of this literacy center. Use expository texts to complement the center so students can seek further information. Change this center to coordinate with a theme, or include several themes to allow for multiple investigations.

Setup

- Create several tubs with various materials and books so students can pursue their own interests. Include actual samples, plastic animals, models, newspaper and magazine articles, and information cards. Have students explore the materials and then compile a short written piece about something they learned. The following are examples of science tub topics:

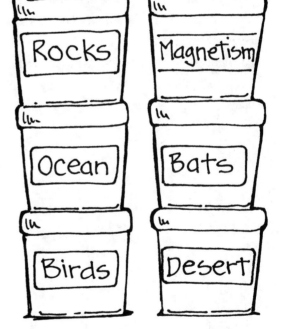

Rocks	Plants/Seeds
Trees	Rain Forest
Desert	Whales
Fish	Amphibians
Dinosaurs	Reptiles
Mammals	Birds
Earth	Solar System
Moon	Skeleton/Bones
Food/Nutrition	Circulatory System
Magnets	Simple Machines
Insects	Arachnids

- Staple multiple copies of the Science Journal reproducible (page 138) into a folder for each student. Have students decorate their folder and title it *My Science Journal*.
- Create experiment stations complete with all the materials necessary to perform science-related activities.
- Provide direct instruction on how to use, clean, and store all materials in the Science Center.

Management

- Have students complete an order form to request materials for independent experiments.
- Enlist parents' help in gathering materials for the center.
- Provide a tub/container where items that need to be washed can be placed.
- Model how to use, how to take care of and carry, and how to put away any fragile, intricate equipment (e.g., microscope, magnifiers).
- Keep a clipboard at the center where consumable items can be recorded to make replacing them quick and easy, or use the Supply List reproducible (page 135) to help with this.

Additional Tip

- Link this center with the Listening/Recording Center for a music connection.

Activities
Verbal/Linguistic

- Have students complete a series of Science Journal reproducibles (page 138) for an experiment that progresses over time (e.g., plant growth, life cycles). Recognize thoughtfully done work in front of the class.

- Have students prepare an oral presentation to explain the steps they took to complete a science experiment.

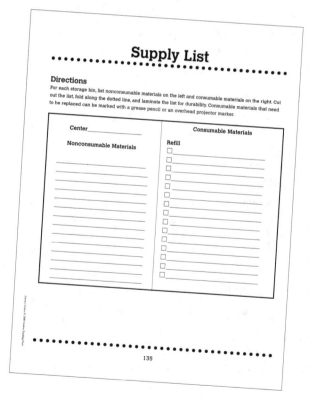

Visual/Spatial

- Have students use center time to create a chart, a skit, or a videotaped presentation to demonstrate knowledge learned during a science lesson.

- Have students create visual/artistic products (e.g., murals, models, collages) that demonstrate their understanding of important concepts. For example, as part of a plant unit, students could create a mural that shows the parts of plants. Or, invite students to create models of a molecule after they have studied this concept.

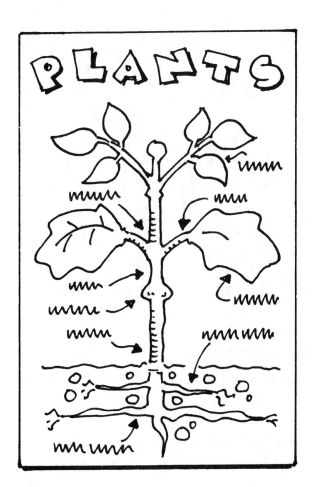

Bodily/Kinesthetic

- Have students pose their own problems and design experiments based on the scientific method (i.e., problem, materials, hypothesis, procedure, and conclusion) to test their problems.

Logical/Mathematical

- Have students read and interpret charts and graphs or create charts and graphs to convey information.

Interpersonal

- Create science "conversation cards" by writing a science fact and a related open-ended question on each card on the Science Conversation Cards reproducible (page 139). Invite members of each group to take turns reading a card and then discussing the question as a group. Have students take turns as the "recorder" who summarizes the discussion on lined paper.

Intrapersonal

- Challenge students to write and present their thoughts on how a topic directly impacts their lives and future. Invite students to find creative ways (e.g., through art work, dramatization, or poetry) to express their own thoughts.

Musical/Rhythmic

- Have students use music to teach their classmates about a science topic. Ask students to write what they want to communicate about that topic, and then have them use those notes to write a song about that subject. Have students tape-record their song and share it at the end of center time.

Naturalistic

- If applicable, have students consider the conservation of a plant, an animal, a habitat, or an ecosystem they are studying. Ask them to research materials and practices that are harmful to it. Then, have them research materials and practices that benefit it. Invite them to present their findings to the class, or have an Environment Night in which students each make a short presentation to invited friends and families in the classroom.

Resources

150 Science Experiments by Barbara Taylor (Barnes & Noble Books)

175 Science Experiments to Amuse and Amaze your Friends by Brenda Walpole (Random House)

Geography

Primary Objective

Students will read a wide variety of sources for the purpose of learning about the world.

Geography is often a neglected area in the curriculum. Give students the opportunity to learn a great deal about the world through a carefully constructed Geography Center using maps and globes and researching areas of interest. Organize this center around continents, countries, regions, states, and/or landforms.

Setup

- Fill tubs with books (fiction and nonfiction), maps, postcards or photos, travel brochures, plastic animals, spices, flags, products, and other items that represent a specific location.

- Locate the Geography Center near bulletin boards so you can post various types of maps for students to use as a reference.
- Include colored pushpins at the center so students can mark locations on maps.
- Posters, globes, and mini-3D-puzzles (e.g., Eiffel Tower, Leaning Tower of Pisa, Big Ben) add visual appeal to this center.
- Laminate map activities from weekly student publications (e.g., *Weekly Reader*, *Scholastic News*, and *TIME for Kids*) for students to complete at this center.

Management

- Build this center over time, or present it in its entirety. Decide which approach would work best based on the nature of your curriculum.
- Use clear tubs to hold and organize materials. Share tubs with other teachers at your grade level to optimize storage space.

Activities
Verbal/Linguistic

- Have students write to different states and/or countries to request materials to place at this center.

- Have students complete a Geography Journal reproducible (page 140) for each tub they have explored. Have students select a location from a geography tub, locate the place on a world map, draw the outline of the region, and draw the flag (if applicable). After students have browsed through the information in the tub, have students write three to five research questions about that area. Then, have students research their area and record the facts they learned on lined paper. Have students staple their Geography Journal reproducible to their lined paper when they have completed their work. Combine the journal pages into a class book.

- Have students make question cards to use with maps. For example, students could write

   Find 3 places you would like to visit.

   Find 3 different landforms.

   Find the northernmost place.

   Find the point with the highest elevation.

   Have students write their questions on index cards and place the cards in a container at the center. Invite students to use the center resources to try answering each other's questions.

Visual/Spatial

- After students have researched several kinds of maps, have them create a map of an imaginary location on the My Map reproducible (page 141). Have students include a key for their map. Use the maps as part of a bulletin board display.

- Find the on-line Web site for your local chamber of commerce. Read through the site, writing down comprehension questions as you go. Bookmark it and invite students to complete your "scavenger hunt" by exploring the site and answering your questions. Then, do the same for other sites such as those for a city hall or tourist bureau.

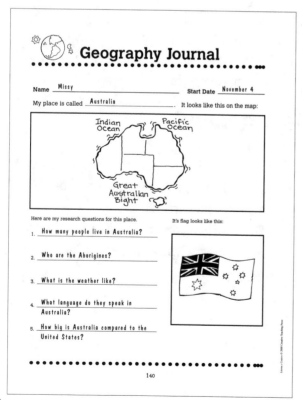

- Tie research tubs in with favorite children's literature such as *Letters from Felix* by Annette Langen and Constanza Droop (Abbeville Press). Introduce the Geography Center by creating research tubs/baskets for the places Felix visited (i.e., Great Britain, France, Italy, Egypt, Kenya, and New York). During the holidays, use *Felix's Christmas Around the World* to help students explore holiday traditions from around the world.

- Have students make an individual or class landform book in which they define and illustrate major types of landforms. Place the book in the Geography Center. Throughout the year, while students investigate different areas, have them find specific places where these landforms exist. Ask students to record the name of the area on a sticky note and place it on the appropriate page in the landform book for you to check before it becomes a permanent part of the book.

- After students have read travel brochures and analyzed their contents, have them design and create a travel brochure for a place they have researched or are learning about.

Bodily/Kinesthetic

- Have students use clay to create relief maps. Invite students to label each area of their map with a flag made from a toothpick and masking tape. Have them fold a piece of masking tape over the toothpick and use a marker to write the landform or area name on the tape.

Logical/Mathematical

- Have students write directions for getting from place to place based on maps from different places (e.g., state, city, mall, theme parks).

- Ask students to sort maps according to their type (e.g., physical, political).

- Have students use precipitation/climate charts and maps for targeted geographical areas to analyze and interpret weather information (e.g., What is the highest average temperature for Brazil in July?).

Interpersonal

- After creating some research tubs, have students work in pairs, choose a tub, and begin their research. Create tubs for geographic areas mentioned in other content areas, including students' classroom reading or continents, oceans, regions, or states. Assemble items and reading material related to the subject.

Average Temperatures for July

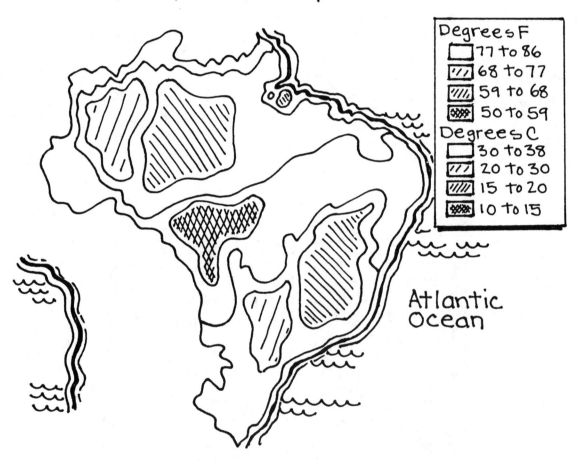

Resources

50 States (Fandex Family Field guides) by Thomas J. Craughwell (Workman Publishing)

Celebrate the 50 States by Loreen Leedy (Holiday House)

Cities of the World series by Deborah Kent or R. Conrad Stein (Children's Press)

The Felix Activity Book by Marc Tyler Nobleman (Abbeville Press)

Felix Explores Planet Earth by Annette Langen (Abbeville Press)

Felix Travels Back in Time by Annette Langen (Abbeville Press)

Felix's Christmas around the World by Annette Langen (Abbeville Press)

From Sea to Shining Sea series by Dennis Brindell Fradin (Children's Press)

Postcards From . . . series by Denise Allard, Helen Arnold, or Zoe Dawson (Steck-Vaughn)

Puzzle Maps U.S.A. by Nancy L. Clouse (Henry Holt & Co.)

The Scrambled States of America by Laurie Keller (Henry Holt & Co.)

True Books series by various authors and editors (Children's Press)

Wish You Were Here: Emily's Guide to the 50 States by Kathleen Krull (Bantam)

Wonders of the World Atlas by Neil Morris (World Book Publishers)

Yo, Sacramento! (And All Those Other Capitals You Don't Know) by Will Cleveland (Millbrook Press)

Art Literacy

Primary Objective

Students will interpret and analyze art and illustrating techniques and demonstrate or enhance their understanding of texts using different art mediums.

Give students an opportunity to engage in a variety of art activities that integrate reading and writing. Use the center to have students learn more about the world of art, including techniques, styles, famous artists, and masterpieces.

Setup

- Whenever possible, locate this center in a place with a large flat area. Countertop space, low tables, or a vinyl tablecloth spread on the floor or over a cluster of desks work well.
- Utilize the resources in your state-adopted art curriculum, if available.
- Use empty egg cartons to hold paint.
- Ask parents to contribute an old shirt for their child to use at the center.
- Hang prints by famous artists and members of the class around the center. Frame both whenever possible. Rotate student artwork through the frames.

Management

- Materials should be organized and stored in labeled containers.
- Teach cleanup procedures.
- It may be helpful to take apart the "How to Draw or Doodle" books (see Resources, page 89) and/or copy pages and laminate them for use in this center. More students can have access to them.

Additional Tip

- This center can also be used as a Reading Response Center in which students respond to text by creating products that reflect their understanding. It can also be used as an extension of the Writing Center where students illustrate their published works.

Activities
Verbal/Linguistic

- Feature an Artist of the Month. Have students read about the famous artist and then analyze his or her work and write a report on the artist. (See Resources, page 89.)

- Present a new piece of art during each center cycle. Select pieces from various forms of art (e.g., sculpture, ceramics, painting, sketch art). Place photographs of the piece of art, a replica, or a computer printout of it. (There are many Web sites geared to adults that show important works of art and give valuable information about the artist and the piece. Print a copy of the artwork, and summarize what makes that piece special for students.) Invite students to write a critical review of the piece. Publish the reviews in an Art Response newsletter, and share the critiques with parents.

Visual/Spatial

- Have students use this center to illustrate individually published books from a Writer's Workshop or to illustrate class books.

- Have students simulate certain illustration techniques (e.g., Eric Carle's tissue paper collage, Ezra Jack Keats' collage technique, Leo Lionni's torn paper technique). Include copies of these illustrators' titles for reference.

- Introduce different art mediums (e.g., watercolor, clay, pastel, crayon resist), and have students use a particular medium to respond to their reading (e.g., make a product that reveals their knowledge of the characters or story).

- Have students use the directions in the "How to Draw" books to create their own illustrations. (See Resources, page 89.)

- Have students complete squiggle pages. Draw random squiggle marks (one per page), and either make each student a Squiggle Book or put copies of squiggle pages at the center one at a time. Invite students to turn the page any way they want and make the squiggle into something by adding details. Have students title their squiggle and write a caption for it.

Bodily/Kinesthetic

- Have students create origami based on the directions in a published book. (See Resources, page 90.)

- Provide students with information about various periods in history. Integrate this information by having students create products that reflect different time periods. For example, students could create illuminations to represent the Middle Ages and hornbooks for the colonial times.

- Have students read books about mixing colors and then explore mixing colors with finger paint or water and food coloring. Invite students to dip coffee filters in colored water to see the results.

Intrapersonal

- Feature a new masterpiece during each center cycle. Have students analyze the masterpiece and respond to it in writing. The following questions will assist students in their analysis:

  What kind of feelings and/or thoughts do you have as you view this masterpiece?

  Why do you think it's considered a masterpiece?

  Why did the artist create this masterpiece? What thoughts or feelings do you think the artist had while creating it?

  What materials did the artist use?

  Where is the masterpiece on display?

Resources

Masterpieces and Famous Artists

Art for Children series by Brigette Baumbusch (Stewart, Tabori & Chang)

A Child's Book of Art by Lucy Micklethwait (DK Publishing)

Come Look with Me: Enjoying Art with Students by Gladys Blizzard (Thomasson-Grant & Howell)

Famous Artists series by various authors (Barron's Juveniles)

Getting to Know the World's Greatest Artists series by Mike Venezia (Children's Press)

I Spy: An Alphabet in Art by Lucy Micklethwait (Greenwillow)

Leonardo da Vinci by Ibi Lepscky (Barron's Juveniles)

Pablo Picasso by Ibi Lepscky (Barron's Juveniles)

People in Art by Anthea Peppin (Milbrook Press)

Start Exploring Masterpieces (coloring book) by Mary Martin (Running Press)

How to Draw Books

Build a Doodle books by Beverly Armstrong (The Learning Works)

Cartoon Book 2 by James Kemsley (Scholastic)

Draw Insects by D. C. Dubosque (Peel Productions)

Ed Emberley's Great Thumbprint Drawing Book by Ed Emberley (Little Brown and Company)
Also:
    Ed Emberley's Drawing Book of Animals
    Ed Emberley's Drawing Book of Faces
    Ed Emberley's Drawing Book: Make a World

How to Draw Boats, Trains, and Planes by Michael LaPlaca (Troll Communications)

How to Draw Dinosaurs by Michelle Roberts (Dover)

How to Draw Portraits in Colored Pencil from Photographs by Lee Hammond (North Light Books)

How to Draw Prehistoric Animals by Linda Murray (Troll)

Superdoodle series by Beverly Armstrong (The Learning Works)
    Dinosaurs
    Mammals
    Insects
    Marine Life
    Reptiles
    200 Animals

Mixing Colors
Color by Ruth Heller (Puffin Books)

The Colors by Monique Felix (American Education Publishing)

Little Blue and Little Yellow by Leo Lionni (Mulberry)

Mouse Paint by Ellen Stoll Walsh (Voyager Picture)

Origami
Holiday Origami by Jill Smolinski (Lowell House)

Horrorgami: Spooky Paper Folding for Children by Steve and Megumi Biddle (Barrons Juveniles)

Planet Origami by Steve Biddle (Barrons Juveniles)

The Usborne Book of Origami by Kate Needham (EDC Publications)

# Overhead Projector

Primary Objective

Students will use an overhead projector to read and reread to build fluency, develop comprehension skills, expand vocabulary, and extend decoding skills.

The use of an overhead projector as a center allows students to engage in a variety of literacy activities such as making words, practicing skills via worksheets, reading familiar poems, and retelling stories. Increase student motivation by using materials on the overhead and inviting students to share their thought processes with each other.

Setup

- Store transparency pens in labeled juice cans, place the cans in the pockets of an apron, and tie the apron around the base of an overhead projector cart or a table.
- Use the overhead projector on a cart, a short table, or the floor. If you use it on the floor, place masking tape in a square to indicate the projector placement. Shine the overhead on a chalkboard, plain chart paper, a dry erase board, or a light-colored surface of some kind.
- Provide a spray bottle of water and tissues for cleanup.
- Make letter tiles for the overhead by typing out uppercase and lowercase letters in a large, clear font on the computer, printing the letters out on a transparency, and cutting apart each letter. Or, purchase a commercially produced set of letters.

Management

- Keep transparencies in sleeves in a three-ring binder organized by categories (e.g., math, handwriting, poems, writing prompts, worksheets). To help students return each transparency to the correct sleeve, also keep a blackline copy in it.
- Frequently model cleanup procedures.
- Rather than putting all of the letter tiles out at once, you may want to choose the ones that students need to complete specific words plus a few extras. Store letter tiles in a labeled container—empty wet-wipe containers work well.
- The work at this center provides wonderful practice but is difficult to grade. It is best to give students a week or two to practice a skill at the Overhead Projector Center and then give a "paper-pencil grade" to the whole group on a similar worksheet.

Activities
Verbal/Linguistic

- Have students choose familiar poems from a collection of shared reading poetry or choose original poems composed by themselves or their classmates. Have students copy the poems onto an overhead transparency and practice reading it on the overhead projector.

- Have students choose poems and then discuss rhyming patterns or words, highlight interesting words, or "capture" words as they read. Show students how to capture a word by putting an index card or sentence strip piece up to the screen and slowly pull it forward. The word will appear to lift off the surface.

- Have students use poems to play I Spy. For example, a student might say *I spy a three-syllable word that is a noun* as a clue.

- Have students work together to review a writing prompt and figure out the type of writing needed to address the prompt. Then, ask students to "capture" the key words that provide this information.

- Create passages with grammatical and spelling mistakes. Have each student in the group assume a different editing role. For example, the student with the red pen corrects capitalization errors. The student with the green pen corrects spelling errors. The student with the blue pen corrects punctuation errors. The student with the black pen corrects usage errors.

- Photocopy a piece of text on an overhead transparency, and cut the text into several sections. Have students read the pieces and place them in logical order on the overhead.

- Have students use transparency letter tiles to make words that fit a pattern or contain a specific combination of letters. Then, have them record 10–15 of their words on lined paper.

* from "Earthquake," from *Angels Ride Bikes/Los Ángeles Andan en Bicicleta* by Francisco X. Alarcón

Visual/Spatial

- Have students complete worksheets that have been printed on transparencies. Invite students to use transparency pens to record their answers. If you use the overhead with the chalkboard or a dry erase board, have students record their answers on these surfaces. Have at least two students work together on this activity.

- Have students practice cursive handwriting using the overheads that accompany a handwriting textbook, if available. Otherwise, write each handwriting exercise on a piece of handwriting paper. Copy the exercises onto an overhead transparency for students to use at the center.

- Have students use spelling words or titles of books to play Hangman. Once a word is guessed, have the student guessing the word use it in a sentence. When a title is guessed, have the student who thought of the title give a summary of the book.

Bodily/Kinesthetic

- Have students use the directions in a book on hand shadows to make different shadows. Invite students to create a story using their hand shadow characters.

- Have students use silhouette puppets that represent key characters to retell or create stories to present to the class. Have students cut out shapes from tagboard that look like the characters and tape them onto clear straws.

Logical/Mathematical

- Have students work together to solve math story problems and/or circle with transparency markers the key words that clue them into the kind of operation that is necessary for solving the problem.

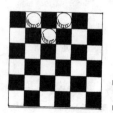

Puzzles and Games

Primary Objective

Students will follow directions and engage in problem-solving strategies to complete puzzles and games.

Have students work together at this center to learn about fair play and winning and losing as they play games together. Encourage students to challenge themselves with individual puzzles and games. Carefully select the puzzles and games for this center. Choose challenging puzzles and games, and combine them with a reading or writing activity.

Setup

- Begin the center with a few games that are familiar to students. Introduce each new game and clearly explain it unless the student objective is to read and follow instructions.

- List each crossword puzzle and other paper-pencil word puzzles on a piece of paper, and make a copy of the list for each student. Glue the list to the inside of each student's file folder. Have students find their folder at the center and sign next to each puzzle or game as it is completed.

- Reinforce game boxes with book tape so they will last longer.

Management

- Conduct a class discussion about taking turns, winning and losing, and problem solving.

- As a class, create a list of suggestions for handling conflict. Encourage students to refer to this list if problems occur at the center.

- Invite students who know how to play the game to become the "experts."

Activities
Verbal/Linguistic

- Have students play word games such as Scrabble, Hangman, Boggle, Scattegories, Balderdash, and Password.

- Have students complete Word Jumbles, Crossword Puzzles, and Mad Libs. Mad Libs are silly stories in which students fill in parts of speech. If you make your own, duplicate or laminate them for reuse.

- Have students go beyond a simple word search and use dictionaries or encyclopedias to research each word they found. Have them record their findings on a separate piece of paper or on the back of the original puzzle.

- Have students create crossword puzzles, word scrambles, and word searches related to spelling, theme, or content area vocabulary on graph paper.

Bodily/Kinesthetic

- Invite students to create their own folder games, board games, or questions in a game-show format (i.e., players take turns replying to a question) to demonstrate knowledge of a skill or content area.

- Have students work with a partner to play a moving game of I Spy. Invite one student to think of an object in the classroom and then give directions to the other student on how to find it.

 **VIP**

Primary Objective

Students will read a wide variety of sources for the purpose of learning about other people.

After students have been exposed to biographies as a genre and/or conducting research on people, use this center to broaden and extend their knowledge of important people.

Setup

- Store materials in baskets or tubs labeled with the person's name or the category the materials represent. Categories might include athletes, presidents, leaders, explorers, authors, scientists, women, African Americans, and Hispanics. Invite students to choose those they are interested in.
- Display photos of the VIPs to add to the visual appeal of the center.

Management

- Keep materials needed for the reports readily available, and include examples of finished products.
- For grading purposes, develop a rubric with students so they will be clear on the expectations. Post the rubric at the center.
- Use display boards to highlight the activities and expectations at this center.

Activities
Verbal/Linguistic

- Have students choose a biography to read and use the VIP Report reproducible (page 142) to brainstorm sensory words to describe a key moment in that person's life from his or her point of view.

- Have students imagine they have traveled back in time to spend a day with the person they choose to research. Have students write about the day, incorporating the information they have learned from their research.

- After students have researched a person, have them choose a significant event from the person's life and write a journal entry as if they were that person. Label this activity Put Yourself in My Shoes. If you provide prompts (e.g., *You are Thomas Edison the day he invented the lightbulb*), place them in a pair of old shoes.

- Reinforce writing from different perspectives by having students use the Two Points of View reproducible (page 143). Ask students to write from the perspective of the VIP as he or she lives out the event that made him or her famous on the left side of the reproducible. Have students write from the perspective of a spectator, a family member, or a friend watching the important person from the sidelines on the right side.

- Have students write a news article as if they were a reporter covering an important event for which the VIP is famous. Remind students to include who, what, when, where, why, and how pieces of information.

Visual/Spatial

- Integrate social studies themes into this center to highlight important people of a particular era or event (e.g., Civil War) or categories of important people that span several eras (e.g., explorers).

- Use the center to feature a theme that will span the entire year, a semester, or for a grading period (e.g., Presidents of the United States, sports figures).

- Model how to research and create a timeline for a person's life. Then, have students read about a person and develop a timeline for his or her life.

- Have students make a trading card for the person they have studied. Ask students to gather important information about the person's life and then condense and record it on the back of an index card. Have students draw a picture of the person on the front of the card.

Bodily/Kinesthetic

- Have students select a famous event in history. Invite them to research the people involved in the event and what role they played. Have students create a short skit to illustrate the event. Invite each student to play the part of one of the famous individuals involved. Invite groups to perform their skit for the class.

Interpersonal

- Have students complete a Famous Person Journal reproducible (page 144) after they have used at least three sources to research the person. Invite students to complete a reproducible for several famous people and staple the pages together to create a journal.

- Feature three to five people (e.g., Five Famous African Americans) at this center, and have students use encyclopedias, biographies, the Internet, and any other available resources to research one of the people. Then, have students work as partners to discuss similarities and differences between their famous people and record this information on a Venn Diagram reproducible (page 128).

Intrapersonal

- Copy some quotations from famous people on large index cards. Have students choose one card, interpret the meaning of the quote, and then apply the quote to their own lives.

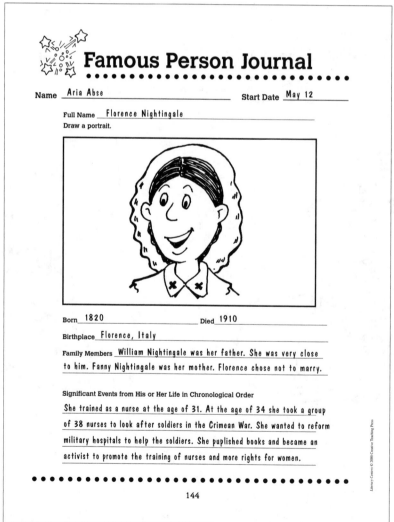

Famous Person Journal

Name _Aria Abse_   Start Date _May 12_

Full Name _Florence Nightingale_

Draw a portrait.

Born _1820_   Died _1910_

Birthplace _Florence, Italy_

Family Members _William Nightingale was her father. She was very close to him. Fanny Nightingale was her mother. Florence chose not to marry._

Significant Events from His or Her Life in Chronological Order

She trained as a nurse at the age of 31. At the age of 34 she took a group of 38 nurses to look after soldiers in the Crimean War. She wanted to reform military hospitals to help the soldiers. She puplished books and became an activist to promote the training of nurses and more rights for women.

144

98

Resources

Childhood of Famous Americans series by various authors (Aladdin Books)
    Abigail Adams
    Mary Todd Lincoln
    Martha Washington
    Elizabeth Blackwell
    Tom Jefferson
    Albert Einstein
    Teddy Roosevelt
    Martin Luther King, Jr.

Famous People by Kenneth & Valerie McLeish (Troll Associates)

Incredible Quotations by Jacqueline Sweeney (Scholastic)

Presidents (Fandex Family Field Guides) by various authors (Workman Publishing)

Step-Up Biographies series by various authors (Random House)

Women in Profile series by various authors (Crabtree Publishing Company)

Center Icons 1

Center Icons 2

Center Icons 3

Literacy Centers © 2000 Creative Teaching Press

Center Icons 4

Center Icons 5

Skills Checklist

● ●

Teacher _____ Year _____

Skill	Whole Group	Small Group	Literacy Center	Other	Comments

√ and date under the type of instruction.

● ●

Status of the Class

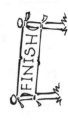

Student	Date	Date	Date	Date	Date	Comments

Literacy Centers © 2000 Creative Teaching Press

Book Talk

Student	Today's Date	Book Title	Assigned Book Talk Date and Time

Checklist

Student

Setting Goals

Name _____ Start Date _____

Date	Reading Goal	Done	Writing Goal	Done

Anecdotal Records

Centers

Name _____

Start Date _____

Directions

Write the names of the centers your group will work at this week in the first column. Write a short summary of what you did at each center on each day. Draw an O in the box if you didn't get to that center.

Name of Center	Day 1	Day 2	Day 3	Day 4	Day 5

Center Checklist

Name _____

Start Date _____

Assignment	Start Date	Finish Date	Comments

112

Literacy Centers © 2000 Creative Teaching Press

Portfolio Piece
Student Selection

● ●

Name _____ Start Date _____

Title of Work _____

I chose this piece for my portfolio because _____

_____

_____

_____ .

The best part about this piece is _____

_____

_____

_____ .

I think I could have made it better if I _____

_____

_____

_____ .

● ●

Portfolio Piece
Teacher Selection

• •

Name _____ Start Date _____

Title of Work _____

I chose this piece because _____

_____

_____

_____ .

I noticed these strengths: _____

_____

_____

_____

I would like you to work on _____

_____

_____

_____ .

• •

Word Families

aud—to hear

audible	audit	auditorium
audience	audition	

graph—to write

autobiography	geography	photograph
bibliography	graphite	telegraph
biography	lithograph	
demographic	phonograph	

mem—remembering

commemorate	memo	memorable
immemorial	memorabilia	

phon—sound

antiphony	microphone	telephone
megaphone	symphony	

tele—far off

telecommunications	telephone	television
telegraph	telescope	

Scavenger Hunt for Word Use

Name _____

Directions

Find and record examples for the categories shown below.

Start Date _____

Nouns	Verbs	Adjectives
Adverbs	An Example of Dialogue	An Example of an Exclamation
		An Example of a Statement
		An Example of a Question

Literacy Centers © 2000 Creative Teaching Press

Scavenger Hunt by Topic

Name _____ Start Date _____

Directions

Find and record examples for the categories shown below.

Topic _____

Literacy Centers © 2000 Creative Teaching Press

Word Sort

Name _____ **Start Date** _____

Directions

Sort your cards into two groups. Describe the pattern you used to sort your words. If you have extra cards, sort them on the back. Glue your finished sort to the paper. Use the back if you run out of room.

Pattern #1 _____   **Pattern #2** _____

_____

Brainstorming 1

Name _____ **Start Date** _____

Directions

Write your topic in the center circle. Write a subtopic in each of the four corner ovals. Write details for each topic in the small circles attached to each oval.

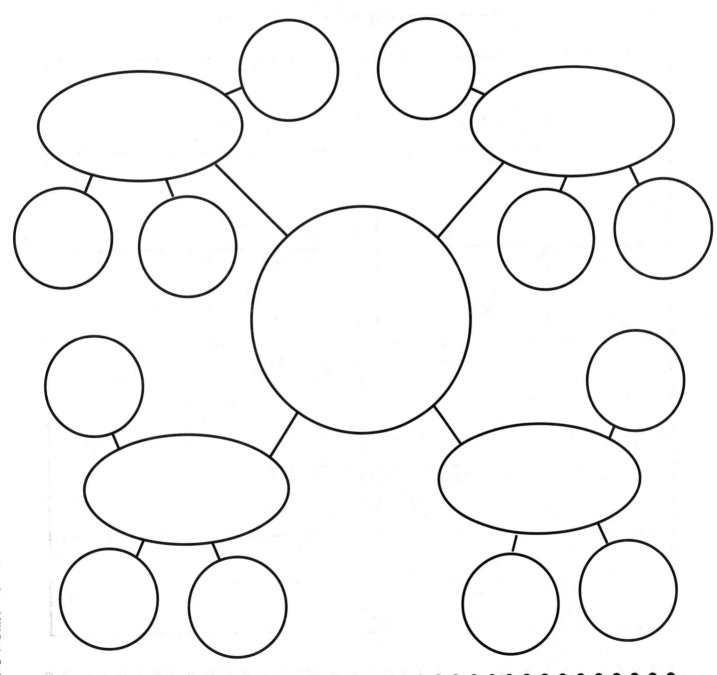

Brainstorming 2

Literacy Centers © 2000 Creative Teaching Press

Name _____   **Start Date** _____

Directions

Write on the lines your main idea, subtopics, and details as indicated.

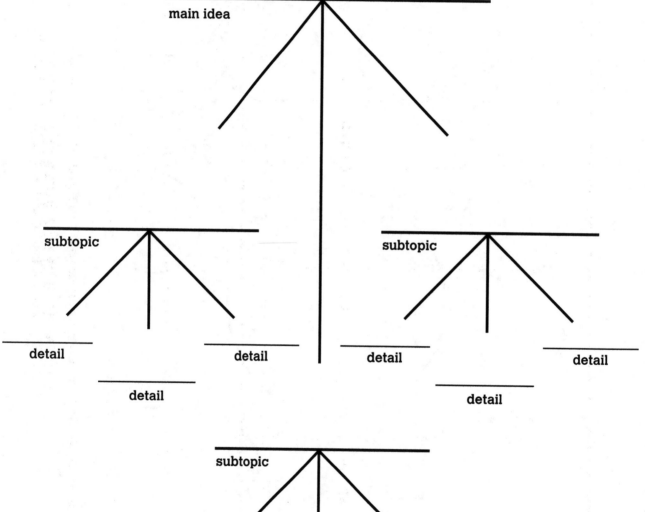

main idea

subtopic

detail

detail

detail

subtopic

detail

detail

detail

subtopic

detail

detail

detail

Brainstorming 3

Directions

Write your topic on the top, center line. Write a supporting idea in each box and list details for each subtopic.

Topic _____

subtopic	subtopic	subtopic	subtopic	subtopic
details	details	details	details	details

Brainstorming 4

Name _____ **Start Date** _____

Directions

Write a sentence or phrase about each element of your story under the appropriate heading.

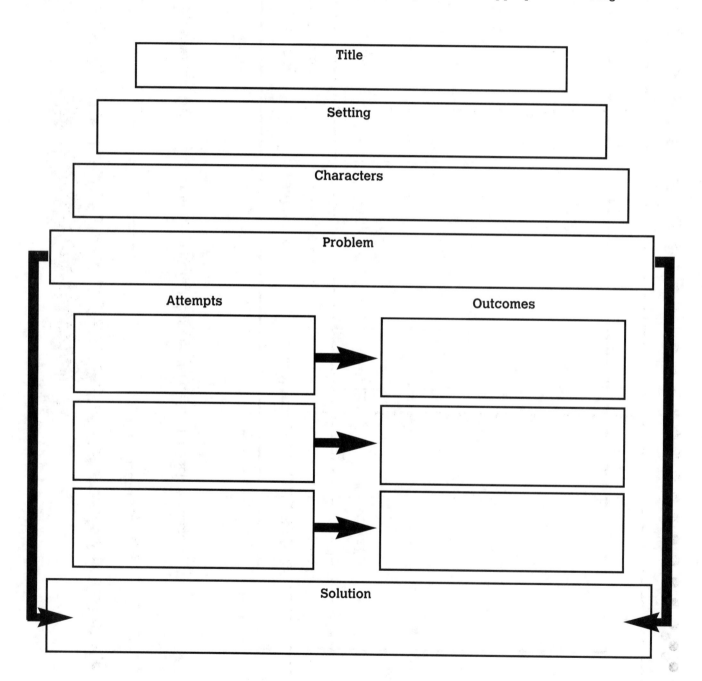

Brainstorming 5

Name _____

Start Date _____

Directions

Write a sentence or phrase about each element of your story under the appropriate heading.

Characters at the Beginning of the Story	Events That Caused Change	Characters at the End of the Story

Turning Point

Most Wanted

Name _____ **Start Date** _____

Draw a picture of your villain.

[ ]

What does your character look like?

_____

_____

What does your character like to do?

_____

_____

What makes your character angry?

_____

_____

What problem does your character create?

_____

_____

Listening Center Log

Name _____   Start Date _____

Date	Title	Counter # at Start	Counter # at End	Comments

Mystery Word Challenge

Name _____   Start Date _____

The Mystery Word is _____ .

I made these words using the Mystery Word letters:

_____   _____

_____   _____

_____   _____

_____   _____

_____   _____

_____   _____

_____   _____

_____   _____

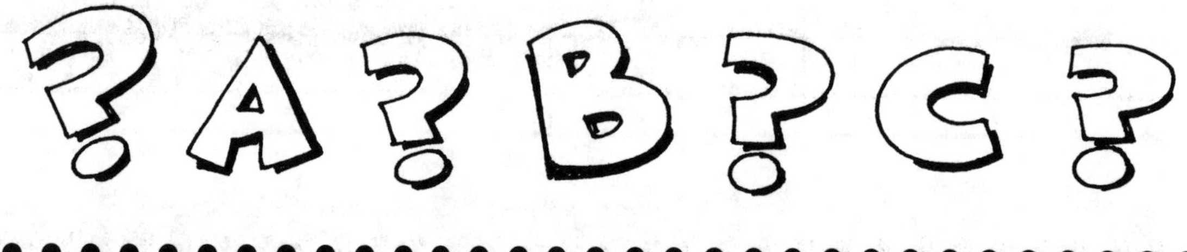

Newspaper Search

Name _____ **Start Date** _____

Directions

Record words you found in the newspaper under the correct heading.

Nouns	Verbs
Adjectives	**Adverbs**
Pronouns	**Conjunctions**

Venn Diagram

Name _____

Start Date _____

Comic Strip

Name _____   Start Date _____

Book Title _____

Directions

Draw a key scene from your book in comic strip format. Don't forget to include dialogue in the form of speech bubbles. Tell why this is an important scene on another piece of paper.

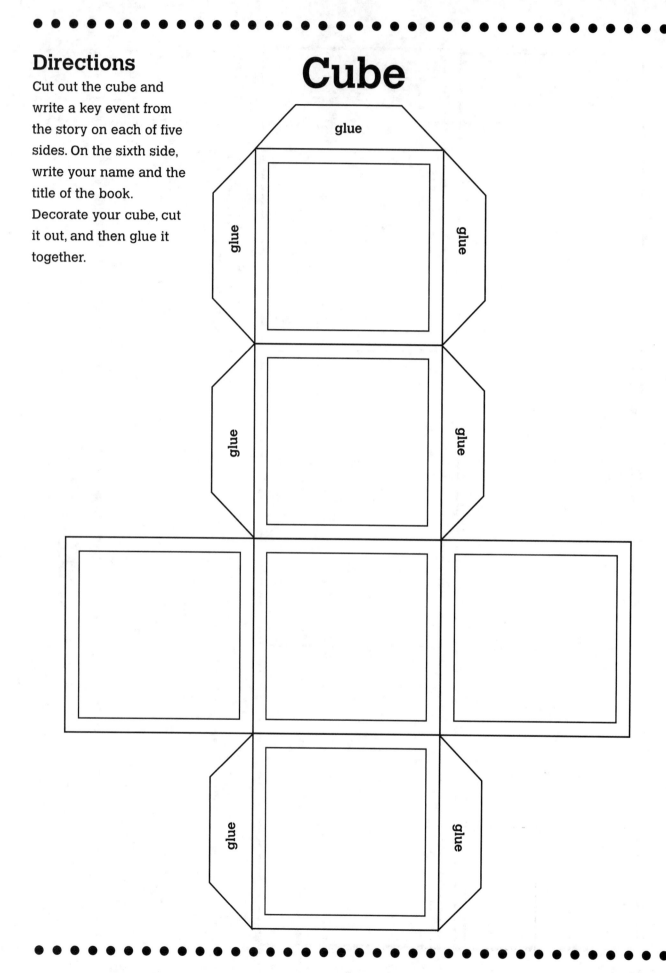

Directions

Cut out the cube and write a key event from the story on each of five sides. On the sixth side, write your name and the title of the book. Decorate your cube, cut it out, and then glue it together.

Cube

glue

glue

glue

glue

glue

glue

glue

Show Time

Students	Today's Date	Presentation Title	Assigned Date and Time

Buddy Reading Form

Partner Reading _____

Partner Evaluating _____

Passage Read _____

One great thing is _____

_____

_____

One thing to work on is _____

_____

_____

Partner Reading _____

Partner Evaluating _____

Passage Read _____

One great thing is _____

_____

_____

One thing to work on is _____

_____

_____

Literacy Centers © 2000 Creative Teaching Press

My Booklist

Name _____ Start Date _____

Date	Title	Goal	Beginning	Ending	Rating

When you have finished reading your book, rate it using the following key:

****   I loved it. It's one of my favorites.

***   I liked it. I would recommend it.

**   It was okay. I'm not sure I would recommend it.

*   I did not like it. I would not recommend it.

New Words

Name _____

Start Date _____

Directions

When you find a new word in your reading, record the word, the name of the book, the page number, the line number, what you think it means, and what the dictionary says it means.

Word	Title of Book	Pg. #	Line #	I think it means	It means

Supply List

Directions

For each storage bin, list nonconsumable materials on the left and consumable materials on the right. Cut out the list, fold along the dotted line, and laminate the list for durability. Consumable materials that need to be replaced can be marked with a grease pencil or an overhead projector marker.

Center_____

Nonconsumable Materials

_____

_____

_____

_____

_____

_____

_____

_____

_____

_____

_____

_____

_____

Consumable Materials

Refill

☐ _____

☐ _____

☐ _____

☐ _____

☐ _____

☐ _____

☐ _____

☐ _____

☐ _____

☐ _____

☐ _____

☐ _____

☐ _____

☐ _____

☐ _____

 # Theme Contract

Name _____ **Start Date** _____

Activity Title _____

Materials I Need to Complete This Activity

_____

_____

_____

Expected Finish Date _____ **Completed** _____

Activity Title _____

Materials I Need to Complete This Activity

_____

_____

_____

Expected Finish Date _____ **Completed** _____

Activity Title _____

Materials I Need to Complete This Activity

_____

_____

_____

Expected Finish Date _____ **Completed** _____

Name _____ Theme Contract page_____

Activity Title _____

Materials I Need to Complete This Activity

_____

_____

_____

Expected Finish Date _____ Completed _____

Activity Title _____

Materials I Need to Complete This Activity

_____

_____

_____

Expected Finish Date _____ Completed _____

Activity Title _____

Materials I Need to Complete This Activity

_____

_____

_____

Expected Finish Date _____ Completed _____

Activity Title _____

Materials I Need to Complete This Activity

_____

_____

_____

Expected Finish Date _____ Completed _____

Science Journal

● ●

Name _____ **Start Date** _____

Topic_____

Tell why this topic interests you.

_____

_____

_____

_____

_____

Illustration

List questions you have

1._____

2._____

3._____

Summarize your findings.

_____

_____

_____

_____

_____

● ●

Science Conversation Cards

Science Conversation Card #____

Fact: _____
_____
_____

Question: _____
_____
_____
_____
_____
_____

Science Conversation Card #____

Fact: _____
_____
_____

Question: _____
_____
_____
_____
_____
_____

Science Conversation Card #____

Fact: _____
_____
_____

Question: _____
_____
_____
_____
_____
_____

Science Conversation Card #____

Fact: _____
_____
_____

Question: _____
_____
_____
_____
_____
_____

 # Geography Journal

Name _____   **Start Date** _____

My place is called _____ . It looks like this on the map:

Here are my research questions for this place.

Its flag looks like this:

1. _____

2. _____

3. _____

4. _____

5. _____

My Map

Name _____

Directions

Draw the outline and key features of your place. Draw and define symbols you use in the Key.

Key

VIP Report

• •

Name _____ **Start Date** _____

Touching Words

Directions

Imagine that you are the person you have been reading about. Pick an important moment in your life and write words that describe what you saw, smelled, tasted, heard, or touched at that moment.

Seeing Words

Topic

Hearing Words

Smelling Words

Tasting Words

Two Points of View

Name _____

Start Date _____

Directions

Under the heading **My Life,** describe your life from the perspective of your VIP as he or she lives out the event that made him or her famous. Under the heading **From the Sidelines,** write about your VIP's life from the perspective of a spectator, a family member, or a friend watching the important person from the sidelines.

My Life

From the Sidelines

Famous Person Journal

Name _____   **Start Date** _____

Full Name _____

Draw a portrait.

```
┌─────────────────────────────────────────────┐
│                                               │
│                                               │
│                                               │
│                                               │
│                                               │
│                                               │
│                                               │
│                                               │
│                                               │
│                                               │
└─────────────────────────────────────────────┘
```

Born _____ **Died** _____

Birthplace _____

Family Members _____

_____

Significant Events from His or Her Life in Chronological Order

_____

_____

_____

_____